THE SUNDAY TIMES

How to Manage Organisational Change

SECOND EDITION

D E Hussey

KOGAN PAGE | *CREATING SUCCESS*

First published in 1995
Second edition 2000

Kogan Page Limited
120 Pentonville Road
London N1 9JN

British Library Cataloguing in Publication Data

A CIP record for this book is available from the British Library.

ISBN 0 7494 3251 9

Typeset by Jean Cussons Typesetting, Diss, Norfolk
Printed and bound in Great Britain by Clays Ltd, St Ives plc

contents

preface

The different types of change, and the various ways of dealing with them, are described in Chapters 1 to 6. Because there are different situations and different choices that can be made, there is a great deal to think about.

The discussion is further developed in Chapter 7 to cover the situation where corporate-wide changes would result from something lower level managers might want to undertake within their own departments.

Chapter 8 provides a form of decision path, to help lead quickly to the appropriate approach. It may be read first if desired, although the detailed explanations and definitions appear in the preceding chapters.

Although my own experience lies behind this book, and the presentation of the approaches is my own, it does, however, owe a great deal to the concepts developed by others. I found inspiration in all the books and articles quoted in the reading list, and should particularly like to acknowledge a debt to the work of Noel Tichy and Mary Anne Devanna, whose concepts of the transformational leader stand behind much of the modern writing on leadership. Also important in shaping my own thinking is the situational approach of Stace and Dunphy, and some of the work of Nadler and Tushman. It owes much to the flow of articles in the journal *Strategic Change*, which I edited for eight years, and to discussions with friends and colleagues. The EASIER model could not have been built without the stimulation of these many ideas.

strategies for change

change is always with us

Change is one of the most critical aspects of effective management. The turbulent business environment in which most organizations operate means that not only is change becoming more frequent, but that the nature of change may be increasingly complex, and it is often more extensive. Many of the change situations that a manager may be involved in are incremental rather than fundamental, and although there is some common ground, there are also differences in how these two types of situation should be managed. These differences will be discussed in this chapter, but at present all that is needed is a reminder that as change situations are different, the response should vary with the situation. There is no single formula that will work in all situations.

Badly handled change situations can lead to serious consequences, which may include:

■ The frustrations of otherwise sound strategies. Research (some of which will be discussed later) suggests that many planned strategies are never implemented, often because the change process is badly managed. This can lead to extra costs, missed opportunities, and sometimes damage to the existing activities of the organization.

▇ The costs of implementation may rise. Delays, spoilt work and emergency action to reduce the impact of delay all add to costs. This is very obvious in large engineering projects, such as the underground railway extension to the Millennium Dome. This project is (at the time of writing) running so far behind schedule that many observers believe that even with all the extra cost and effort put into it, it may still not be completed in time for January 2000. Although it may be less noticeable, bad implementation may lie behind many other types of change failure. For instance, the TQM initiative that still disappoints after the second attempt; or the new organizational structure that is dependent on a new computer system and results in an increase of costs instead of the promised reduction. Consider the problems in 1999 in the Passport Office, where staff were reduced in anticipation of savings from computerization, but then had to be increased again when the system did not deliver its promised value.

---

example: the Passport Office
There can be few people who were living in the UK during 1999 who could be unaware of the problems that beset the Passport Agency when the backlog of unprocessed passport applications reached 565,000. The immediate cause was the failure of a new computerized system to deliver its benefits. However, the National Audit Office in a report on the situation put much of the blame on management failings:

■ Not assessing the time needed for staff to become competent with the new system.

■ Not having any contingency plan in case things went wrong.

■ Inadequate communication with the public.

The National Audit Office estimated the costs of the failure to the public purse as £12.5 million. This included:

■ £6 million on additional staff and overtime payments;

■ £100,000 on compensation to the 500 people who missed holidays because their passports could not be delivered on time;

■ £16,000 on umbrellas to protect the huge crowds queuing at the offices from the rain;

■ and £5,000 on luncheon vouchers for those forced to queue for long periods.

■ Benefits expected from the change may be lost. For example, through competitors getting in first and pre-empting the expected sales gains, or through weaknesses in performance that leave room for them to do a better job in the market, taking a market share that would otherwise have gone to the initiating organization. The converse is true, in that a well-handled change can create a competitive position that may be difficult for competitors to combat. Direct Line, the British insurance company, played havoc with the established insurance companies when it introduced its innovative approach to direct marketing. Its success was partly in the new concept, and partly because it successfully managed the change processes needed to support the strategy and meet the growth it generated. Would it have been successful if customers faced difficulty getting a telephone call through, or if the paper work was often full of errors? Dixons have been successful in introducing Freeserve, a free to the user Internet access service. Some rival firms failed with their similar services because of implementation, as customers gave up once they found it close to impossible to get through to the service, making the Internet inaccessible for all practical purposes.

▪ The human consequences of the change may become greater. The human price when change leads to people losing their jobs is already high, but it becomes much worse when the change is handled carelessly or without adequate planning.

▪ Motivation may be reduced within the organization as people feel the confusion and chaos that often accompany a poor change management situation, and faith is lost in senior management. If you have experienced working in an organization where your colleagues are cynical and disillusioned, you will know what I mean. If you have also worked for an enthusiastic organization you will have seen the contrast for yourself. The difference between the two may be uncontrollable events, but is usually management capability.

▪ Resistance to future changes may increase as people feel that their worst fears about the present change are justified. There are few modern organizations that can make a change to end all changes (unless the change is to close down!), so it is always important to handle each change in the best possible way. Why make things harder for next time?

It may never be possible to make all types of change situation smooth and pleasant experiences for everybody. But it is always possible to approach change situations with care, diagnosing the nature of the change, selecting the best way to plan for it, and implementing those plans. This book is intended to help you be better prepared to deal effectively with the change situations that are an inevitable part of a manager's job.

---

example: the Child Support Agency

The Child Support Agency was set up in April 1993. The information from which this example was drawn comes from official reports by a Parliamentary select committee, the National Audit Office, the Parliamentary Ombudsmen, and various newspaper stories.

The vision behind the Child Support Agency had wide support: that absent fathers who were not giving their children adequate financial provision should take responsibility in the interests of the child, and so that the burden on the state was reduced. Despite this, few people would accept that the implementation of this vision has been a success. The Parliamentary Ombudsman quoted examples of inadequate procedures, failure to answer letters, incorrect or misleading advice, and delays in achieving results in individual cases. Also staff were inadequately trained.

Behind these basic flaws in the implementation of the CSA lie further faults, which can be described as a failure by government to think out in advance the consequences of many aspects of the enabling legislation. The formula for assessing how an absent parent's maintenance contribution should be set led to many injustices, many of which could have been foreseen and prevented. Political pressure for quick results meant that more effort was spent on increasing the contributions of parents who were already making payments than in tracing the many fathers who were making no contribution at all.

The result of this badly handled change was that few children had benefited during its initial two years of operation. Some 350,000 cases, a third of the backlog, were shelved. Public support faltered. The costs of running the agency rose. Originally established with 5,000 employees, it failed to meet its financial targets and has had to increase its staff significantly.

causes of change

There has never been an age in which change has not taken place. Today there is an increase in the unpredictability of many of the factors that cause organizations to change, and an increase in the speed with which organizations have to respond in order to stay in the game. Many organizations appear to be in an almost continuous state of change, and the breathing spaces between one change and another tend to disappear. What are the forces causing this?

- Technological change continues to accelerate, so the speed with which obsolescence occurs is also increasing. Organizations cannot ignore developments that could give advantages to their competitors, and it is only very rarely that a new development can be substituted for an old one without causing changes to skills, jobs, structure and, often, culture.
- Competition is intensifying, and becoming more global. More organizations are compelled to attain the standards of quality and cost achieved by the pacemakers in the industry. More industries are served on a world basis, and in these conditions it is no longer sensible to think in single-country isolation. This significant trend is set to become more significant with the growth of the Internet and E-Commerce.
- Customers are more demanding, and will no longer accept poor service or low quality. To be competitive organizations have to respond more rapidly to customer needs, and these can and do change over time. It is no longer sensible for an organization to ignore the way its customers' needs and expectations are changing, and the wise managers will always try to keep one step ahead. This in turn means that organizations periodically have to change the way that they

interact with customers, which means different structures, systems, culture, and services.

■ The demographic profile of the country is changing. In many EU countries and the United States, the proportion of older people is going up, and that of younger people going down. This will bring continuing pressures on countries and organizations. Topical national issues include the rising burden of pension and healthcare provision, and the possibility of increasing the national retirement age. Corporate issues will include finding ways of dealing with skill shortages, changes in attitudes to the employment of older people, and problems of motivation in flat organizational structures, which offer little opportunity for promotion. Think about what these trends could mean in terms for your organization over the next decade, and you will soon realize that they hide numerous areas where change will occur.

■ Privatization of publicly owned businesses continues, and their monopoly protection disappears. This is a world trend, and even where ownership does not change, new systems are often established to create competition and market forces, as in the National Health Service under the previous Conservative government in the UK. Related to this is the move, which has been very strong through the 1990s, for mutual organizations to de-mutualize. Examples include building societies (Halifax, Woolwich), insurance companies (Clerical Medical, South African Mutual) and others (RAC, AA).

■ Shareholders demand more value. The influence of the money markets on demands for corporate performance, with high proportions of shares residing with institutional investors, creates a pressure for continued improvement in capital growth and earnings. Companies may come under considerable pressure if the markets consider that they are performing below expectations, even though they may be profitable. Marks and Spencer came under such pressure in 1998 not because it was in loss, but because its profitability had slipped. This in turn was the trigger for many changes in activities, structure and procedures in M & S. Another example is British Airways, which in the summer of 1999 announced new plans to shrink its network by 12% over three years to restore its profitability. In such situations pressure comes not just from complaints by major shareholders, but because under-performing companies become targets for take over. There are also financial organizations like Value Active Fund, whose business purpose is to take stakes in under-performing companies in order to persuade other shareholders to support moves such as a merger or break up of the target company.

Typical change situations triggered by these forces include:

- ■ Downsizing, or rightsizing – both expressions mean that organizations are becoming smaller, and structures flatter.
- ■ Approaches that lead to rethinking ways of doing things, such as world-class manufacturing, business process re-engineering and continuous improvement.
- ■ Increases in outsourcing of activities previously handled inside the organization. This is more than a question of finding suppliers, and usually involves a close relationship between the organization and its outsourcing partners.
- ■ Methods that reduce time in the development of new products or activities.
- ■ More organizations become involved in strategic alliances and joint ventures.
- ■ Acquisitions continue to be a key strategic activity.

Added to this are the 'normal' change situations of expansion into different markets, the launch of new products and the numerous incremental changes that are required as managers make adjustments to market needs.

keeping pace with change

At one time the advice given for change management was to follow a freeze–unfreeze–freeze sequence. The idea was to reduce the frequency of change, thereby making it more manageable, and reducing disruption within the organization. During a period when the organization was frozen and no major changes undertaken, things that needed to change would be noted and eventually the time would come when all the changes would be made at once. After the changes had been implemented, everything would be frozen for a further period. Obviously there would be an exception if an organization were in deep trouble, but generally, because much of the change was incremental rather than fundamental, the organization was able to exercise control over when to change. One organization that I know operated in this way in the 1970s was a Swiss based global pharmaceutical company. Every five years there would be a major exercise to examine what changes were needed for the strategic direction of the company, and the structures and processes needed to achieve it. These would be implemented and held firm, with the exception of minor changes, for the full five-year period.

Under modern conditions, events move too fast for this stabilizing approach to change. The result is that many more organizations undertake significant change very frequently, and have to react in a time scale set by the trigger event, rather than having the luxury of choosing to change when the organization feels it is ready.

Something happens inside or outside the organization that is perceived as a trigger event. This gives birth to a need to change to meet the new challenge, which may be an opportunity or a threat. Someone in the organization has to define the change needed, create some sort of vision of the benefits that will result, and make the change work. In the modern organization these trigger events tend to occur too fast for comfort.

Although it is tempting to think of change management as something of interest only to the chief executive, this would be a mistake. Certainly, many of the examples of good or bad management come from major changes that affect whole organizations, but this is because they are well documented and it is more interesting to use as examples organizations that are well known. There remain many changes that have to be managed by people at many levels in the organization. Sometimes the trigger for change might indeed come from the chief executive, but a manager is left to interpret how to make the change work in his or her area of responsibility. Frequently the trigger event may be external, but affecting only a part of the organization, in which case perceiving the need for change and taking the appropriate steps may be a responsibility at any level.

what type of change?

In any change situation the first step is to think about the nature of the change and the situation inside the organization. Although there is some overlapping of approaches, there are differences between what might be termed incremental change and fundamental change. My thinking on the different ways of approaching different change situations owes much to the work of two Australian writers, D A Stace and D C Dunphy (see further reading), who were among the first to suggest that different situations demand different approaches to change management.

Incremental change is almost self-evident, and covers the hundreds of situations that managers face throughout their careers. It includes changes of: work methods and processes; factory layout; new product launches; and other situations where most people would see a continuity from the old state to the new. It is progress by evolution rather than revolution, and although after a long period an observer would see a great difference between the organization as it was and as it now is, no one change makes the whole organization feel very different. This does not suggest that these changes are all easy to implement, nor that there will be no resistance to them.

By contrast, fundamental change means what it says. Other words that have been used to describe this type of change include 'strategic', 'visionary' and 'transformational'. Together they give something of the flavour of this type of change. By definition it makes a noticeable impact on the organization (or that part of the organization undergoing the change). If it is successful, the difference will be noticeable inside and outside of the organization.

Such changes are usually large, dramatically affect the future operations of the organization and frequently involve major upheaval. The results of a business process re-engineering activity that alters the entire way in which a business operates, a merger with another organization, the downscaling of an organization, or the movement of the organization into completely different activities, are all examples of such change.

Among the particular situations that most people will be aware of are: the introduction of Health Trusts in the National Health Service; British Petroleum's Project 1990, which led to downsizing, a major culture change and outsourcing of many activities; the changes going on in the privatized organizations, such as British Gas and British Telecommunications, as they struggle to align culture, structure and operations to the competitive situation. There may be more glamour in fundamental change, but there is also more pain and an enhanced opportunity to do lasting damage to the organization if the change process is handled badly.

You really need to think flexibly when judging whether a

change is fundamental. Assume that you are head of a unit of 25 people in one of the large organizations such as General Electric. A change that affected only your unit would not be fundamental if looked at from the viewpoint of the whole organization. I doubt if the chief executive of GE would even want to know about it. But from your viewpoint and those of the people under you, it may be as fundamental as it can get. What if half the people, as a result of the change, now had the wrong skills and experience, everyone had to change the way in which they operated, and some people were to be relocated to different parts of the world, although still reporting to you? For everyone concerned this is a very far-reaching change, and to make it happen effectively you would have to have change management skills of a very high order.

For both incremental and fundamental change there are two other factors that should be considered, which will affect the approach used to implement the change.

urgency

How urgent is the need for change in relation to the extent of the actions that have to be taken? It may not be very urgent to alter the layout of an office to improve communication and speed the flow of work, but it may still be possible to have these changes in place, long before a highly urgent, complex reorganization and culture change can be finished. Delaying the office layout plan by a month to achieve total commitment of all affected may be a high percentage of the time needed for total implementation but may not be a serious concern for the organization. The same percentage delay on an urgent, complex reorganization, which in any case would take the best part of a year, may be untenable. The greater the need for urgency, the less relaxed the approach to change can be. However, do not forget that change has not happened until the new state is effective, and what appears to be the fastest route –

just ordering people to do the new thing – may actually take longer, for reasons that will be explored later.

resistance

Equally important is the degree of resistance to change. If everyone wants change, the implementation methods may be very different from those chosen when resistance is high. Where the resistance occurs is also important; the higher up the organization this is, the harder it can be to overcome. Resistance might come about for personal reasons, or could be because the people concerned with it do not perceive the need for change. When the liquidator is knocking on the door, most will see the need and although the change may not be welcomed by all, few will argue that nothing needs to be done. Not so when an organization appears to be doing well, and the change is because of top management's recognition of an emerging problem that others have not spotted.

I was tempted to look at another heading, the importance of the change. However, by definition all fundamental changes are important, otherwise few people would attempt them, while the importance of incremental changes is reflected to some degree in the urgency with which they should be made. If importance is zero, then urgency is also zero, and there is little point in the change.

The styles of strategies suggested for handling the various change situations vary from participative to dictatorial, and suggestions are made below for appropriate approaches for each situation. The problem with general advice is that situations are always specific, and certain situational factors should be considered that may modify the approach. The following questions should also be considered.

1. What are the skills and abilities of those affected by the change? Participation may have to be reduced if

the people involved lack the ability to contribute and cannot be brought up to speed quickly. Where lack of ability limits the effectiveness of participation, it may be necessary to substitute extensive and regular communication for total involvement.

2. Are people motivated to participate? The method chosen will also be affected by the willingness of those affected to play a part. Even where resistance to change is low, those affected may not wish to play an active part in determining the scope of the change, or even how to implement the change once it has been decided. When the change is fundamental, such as removing layers of management, motivation may be different at different stages of implementation. In the beginning, uncertainty about who is to leave the organization may increase resistance. Would you feel highly motivated by a change if you thought that you were to be made redundant as a result? Once issues like this have been determined there may be a strong motivation to get the new structure working.

3. Does the suggested approach fit the organization's culture? It may not be impossible to use an approach that goes counter to the normal culture of the organization, but it may sometimes be more effective to modify the approach to achieve a better fit. Extensive participation may be viewed with suspicion in an organization with a boss-powered, fear culture. Equally, a totally dictatorial approach may demotivate if the organization is normally participative. It should be remembered that fundamental change often includes a need to change culture, and, if so, the way in which change is implemented should give consideration to both old and new values.

4. How confidential is the change? Confidentiality is more likely to affect the point where involvement can take place than to prevent it at all. It should not be

used as an excuse for using a less appropriate change strategy over the whole life of the change than would otherwise be desirable. There may be genuine reasons for confidentiality, such as an intention to sell part of the business to another company, where wide disclosure too soon could lead to premature changes to share prices. Sometimes the reasons given are a reflection of the prejudices of the person leading the change. For example, the chief executive of one of my clients believed that factory workers should be kept in ignorance of any issues that might affect the volume of work, on the basis that if they thought work was drying up, they would slow down to avoid possible redundancies. This contrasted dramatically with the view of the chief executive of another client who I was working with at the same time. This chief executive held the opinion that all workers had the right to know the state of the order book in the plant in which they worked, and they were to be updated regularly. The reality was that workers were much more co-operative when changes became necessary in the second company because things had not been concealed from them. If you have to judge whether to exclude people on grounds of confidentiality, make sure that you are considering what is really important.

5. How important is it to retain the loyalty and sustain the motivation of the people affected? In most situations many of the people affected by the change will continue working in the organization, but this is not always the case. For example, it is doubtful whether Rupert Murdoch's organization cared whether the print workers stayed with the organization or left during the forced change of the 1980s, since the whole issue was about new technologies and practices. Although now an old example, it remains a classic. The newspaper industry in the UK was not

very profitable at that time, as it was compelled by the power of the unions to keep existing manning levels even if new labour saving technology was introduced. Consequently there was no gain from technological progress. Modern production methods were available and, largely through computer-based technology, could bring a total change to the economics of the industry, were it not for the union attitudes. In this instance, dictatorial, confrontational change methods were probably the only ones that could work, as over the years others had tried and failed to remove the restrictive practices by agreement. The battle was bitter, with the striking workers being effectively locked out of the printing plant, which they blockaded as replacement workers were brought in. One hopes that in the modern UK, there is more of a spirit of partnership between unions and employers, and that such a situation could be resolved differently if it were to occur again.

6. How many people are affected by the change? Advice given below should be tempered with what you know about the scale of the organization, or that part of it which is undergoing a change. A higher level of participation can be achieved in a shorter period of time in a small organization. All the people in a small business or organizational unit can be involved very quickly, and some of the time constraints discussed below will be less significant. Gaining participation from, say, 30 people who all know each other, is easier than if there are 300. At 3,000 the problem is considerably more complex, and at 30,000 the time needed increases again and the task of achieving participation becomes a project in itself.

incremental change

Figure 1.1 fits what is likely to be the most effective approach to change management to the various circumstances suggested by the matrix. This should be taken as indicative, as the final selection must also consider the factors discussed above.

The matrix suggests clear-cut solutions to clear-cut situations. In practice, the situations are often between the positions shown on the matrix, in which case a blend of approaches is often appropriate.

| | | RESISTANCE | |
		LOW	HIGH
URGENCY	LOW	EXTENSIVE PARTICIPATION	PERSUASIVE
	HIGH	FOCUSED PARTICIPATION	PERSUASIVE or COERCIVE

Note: Choice of approach will be affected by:
1. Skills and abilities of employees
2. Motivation of employees to participate
3. Culture of the organisation
4. Confidentiality of the change
5. Longer-term motivational needs.

Figure 1.1 *Approaches to incremental change*

extensive participation

Where resistance to change is low and the urgency is also low, it should be possible to achieve change through extensive participation, allowing those who would be affected by the change to play a major part in determining what the change should be and how it will be implemented. If it is not possible to involve everyone in determining the change itself, it may be possible to have extensive involvement in how to implement it. One advantage is that matters of detail, which may be unknown to the change leader, are less likely to be overlooked, and a broader view can be taken of the implications of the change. An even greater advantage of extensive participation is that it provides for ownership of the change by those affected, which increases motivation, and makes it more likely that the change will in fact be implemented. The difficulty a manager faces is how to lead the change without becoming too directive, and how to ensure that participation is effective and that discussion does not become a substitute for action. These are points that are dealt with later.

One example of this approach is in the introduction of a new way of planning sales representatives' activities. The manager has collected some factual information about how representatives' time is spent, to identify areas where more could be achieved, and then sets out the objectives of a sales planning system. Instead of defining the whole system at this stage and implementing it by edict, the manager may use sales meetings to create a shared vision of the need to change, and the elements that people agree should go into the system. Everyone is involved in this, and also in defining what else needs to be done to make the system effective (for example, training).

Staff work has to be undertaken to ensure that all aspects of the suggested system are coherent and fully worked out, but again, this may be discussed with the sales representatives. Agreement is reached that the representatives want to apply the approach. Attention is given to the other issues raised, as part of the implementation process.

focused participation

Resistance to change is still low, but the change is urgent. There is not enough time to involve everyone in the change implementation process. This means that a more focused approach is required and the most important task is to identify the people who are critical for the success of the change and to win their participation, at the same time ensuring that there is clear communication with the rest of the people affected. The change leader still has to determine whether the key people are involved in reaching a solution, or whether their involvement should be in how to make that solution work. The former is preferable, and is usually practicable. Key people are not necessarily restricted to levels in the hierarchy, and may also be expanded to include those who have influence in the organization or have information that helps define the change and implement it.

persuasion

Where resistance to change is high and urgency is low, a persuasive approach is suggested. This sets out to convince those concerned of the need for the change and the appropriateness of the solutions. 'Selling' the concept has some appeal to task-oriented managers, and can be effective. More effective, because it fits more situations, is to create a shared vision of the desired state that will result from the change. 'Selling' may lead to disappointment, and increased resistance if the benefits promised are not forthcoming. Shared vision becomes an internal motivation and the same problems that cause rejection after the 'selling' approach may be a spur to further action to find ways round any obstacles. The difference is that 'selling' is a promise, while shared vision is something everyone works to achieve. Once there is agreement about a shared vision, it should be easier to gain commitment first to the need for change, and later to the change itself.

Persuasive methods may also be effective in our last box on the matrix, when both urgency and resistance are high.

coercive methods

There are situations where it is obvious from the outset that a particular group of people are so entrenched in their views that persuasive methods will either not work, or will take too long. In these situations a more coercive approach may be better. This still maintains good communication with those involved, but uses power and pressure to enforce the changes. People are instructed to take certain actions, and sanctions are applied if they do not obey these instructions. There should be no need to cross the borderline between a coercive and a dictatorial approach. The coercive approach will explain the situation, and will listen to feedback (but not for too long), then the manager will decide and expect the decisions to stick. A dictatorial approach is discussed later.

fundamental change

Fundamental change brings more issues to consider. Incremental change is often marginal in its long-term impact on people. Fundamental change can strike at their security, alter the satisfaction achieved from a job, or even remove the job completely. After the change the organization will become something different. Figure 1.2 gives a view of appropriate approaches, but has a different approach to urgency, where the scale varies from high to crisis. A low-urgency change could hardly be considered fundamental. It is hard to conceive of any managing directors deciding to change the culture when the issue is not important, and the change would be implemented slowly whenever they could find the time! What managing director would decide that downsizing was critical for profitability, but that it did not really matter when it was done?

Again, although suggestions can be made for what will frequently be the best approach, what is offered here is purely indicative.

RESISTANCE

	LOW	HIGH
HIGH	VISIONARY/ CHARISMATIC	VISIONARY/ COERCIVE
URGENCY		
CRISIS	VISIONARY/ PERSUASIVE	DICTATORIAL

Figure 1.2 *Approaches to fundamental change*

The word 'visionary' is applied as a prefix to the descriptions in three of the boxes. This is an important emphasis and, although two of the descriptions have been met before, the size and scale of fundamental change mean that reaching a shared vision is both more difficult and more important than it is with incremental change.

visionary/charismatic

When resistance is low, and the organization is not in crisis, the momentum for change may be sustained by the charismatic qualities of the leader. Trust in such a person is likely to be high (or resistance would be higher), and considerable enthusiasm may be generated for the change because of this. Charisma alone will not bring about effective fundamental change and, in addition, attention has to be given to the detail of implementation. I do not know how charismatic the first chief executive of the Child Support Agency was, but it is clear that one reason for the CSA's difficulties was lack of understanding by government of the implications of many of the regulations the CSA had to follow. There is a great deal of planning and administration in managing any form of fundamental change.

visionary/persuasive

When the organization is in crisis then, provided knowledge of this crisis is shared and believed, and resistance to change is low, speed is of the essence. The most important feature of change management in this box is to instil a belief in the future throughout the organization. I have suggested coupling this with a persuasive approach, because the strongest need might be to convince people that the particular direction selected is the right one.

visionary/coercive

Where resistance is high and the organization is not in crisis, a coercive approach may be the most appropriate. Time may not be available for extensive participative or persuasive approaches. The visionary emphasis is just as important as in the other two situations, because the need is to come through the change situation with a united organization, which means that the leaders must create confidence throughout the organization that they know what they are trying to achieve. Where the organization cannot be led, it must be driven.

dictatorial

When the ship is heading for disaster, and the crew appears to have no sense of purpose, the only methods likely to work quickly are those that give orders and apply discipline where they are ignored. This sort of change process can be littered with management casualties, as those offering the most resistance are neutralized. It is often seen in an acquisition situation, where the acquirer has a need to demonstrate speedy results from the purchase, and particularly when the company bought has had a recent poor performance, although often a somewhat less draconian approach might work better for the long term.

However, where achieving results now is essential for survival, this is more critical than any damage to long-term morale. In these circumstances the only vision is to survive!

help from Jane Austen

When thinking of approaches to change management, it is worth remembering that if it fits the situation, participation is likely to yield better long-term results than persuasion, and persuasion is preferable to coercion. Four words that might be kept in mind when selecting the right approach are:

- Pride. Do not feel too proud to involve others, as this does not imply weakness on your part. Misplaced pride could lead to your using an autocratic approach when participation would achieve better results. However, participation does not involve abdication, and calls for a higher level of managerial leadership than order giving.
- Prejudice. Examine your prejudices when considering a change situation. Managers often make comments such as, 'They could not help as they do not have the right knowledge.' Check that this is not just an assumption that has become a prejudice.
- Sense. In all management activities common sense has a great part to play. Books such as this can suggest ways of tackling change and give detailed guidance on methods, but in any situation you are there and the author of the book is not. So ensure that all advice is given a common-sense check before you decide to follow it.
- Sensibility. Many forms of change can hurt people, and this is particularly true of fundamental change. Sensitivity to other people's feelings may not always seem important, but it separates good managers from the poor ones. Change that causes people to lose their

jobs is often unavoidable, but the way in which this is done is often unacceptable. Tact and consideration are important to those who are staying, as well as those who are leaving.

In the following chapters we will look at some approaches that are particularly helpful in planning change, explore the causes of resistance to change, and examine leadership of change. As the chapters progress, the need for detailed thought at each stage will be emphasized.

what can be learnt from the CSA case?

As a preview of the issues to be considered later, let us look at some of the probable causes of poor change management in the CSA example.

■ Vision. The vision became less clear than was first thought, and some of the actions initiated appeared to owe more to the desire of the Treasury to save money than to the other aim of improving the lot of children. Emphasis of only one part of the vision led to actions that lost the CSA considerable public support, and opened the door to those who were opposed to it.

■ Pre-planning. It is necessary to think through the probable consequences of any change. The more fundamental the change, the more complex are the logical consequences. The fact that the formula for assessing parental maintenance was flawed and unjust was the fault of those who planned the change, not the agency set up to implement it. Also underestimated was the difficulty of persuading fathers to accept assessments that they felt were both unjust and unaffordable.

■ Implementation. The Ombudsman drew attention to poor procedures and lack of training of new staff. Making change work is as important as deciding where to change. It is a critical element of the overall change process, and applies whatever the nature of the change. When change is complex, it is not an easy task.

why change might be resisted

people and change

It is a popular myth that humans always resist change. This myth defies historical fact, for humans have always been the most adaptable of animals. In fact, a measure of change is often welcomed because it brings excitement. Few people would like to work in organizations where nothing different ever happened, yet at the same time we all know of situations where change has been resisted, and made harder to effect because of this resistance.

Obviously, there are differences between people. One person may be more averse to risk than another. Another may find it difficult to see the benefits of the change, although a colleague may be enthusiastic. Differences such as this will always exist, and only rarely will the reactions of just a few individuals frustrate the management of change, unless they are in a position of power or influence.

Many forms of incremental change cause no resistance at all, the advantages being readily apparent. Salespeople, for example, rarely object if they are given a new, relevant product to sell. Expanding sales into a new market may be stimulating and exciting. Other incremental changes may cause more concern. The new layout of the factory, which moves a workstation to the opposite side of the building, may be upsetting for the individual. However, managers may not see that there is any difference to the job and its tasks, and may therefore fail to understand that there could be a reason for concern. Similarly, valued informal group relationships may be broken if a change to the organizational structure shifts people from one unit to another, even if their jobs remain the same.

Fundamental change may bring well-founded fears of redundancy, different ways of working that cut across the experience of years, or changes in responsibility. These can be readily understood because the implications are visible. We all know that we would feel threatened if our own unit was being downsized. We may not find it so easy to see that a change of procedures that does not affect the income of the individual can also be seen as a threat. And when we ourselves welcome empowerment that gives us more freedom of initiative and more responsibility for our own actions, we may find it hard to accept that others are not of the same mind. The first stage in developing ways of reducing resistance is to understand it. Although thinking 'How would I feel if this were happening to me?' may increase your sensitivity to the impact of change, the real issue is deeper than this: it is how the people affected by the change would feel.

the psychological contract

One concept I have found useful is that of the 'psychological contract'. Many conditions of employment are spelt out in formal documents that make the rewards clear. These define salaries, whether overtime is paid, what holidays we get, the hours of attendance and similar matters. But this is not all that one expects from a job.

The psychological contract covers the unwritten and almost subconscious elements of the relationship. It covers the things that individuals gain from the job, and things that they are expected to provide in return. An important part of the benefit might be being able to work on one's own initiative, the opportunity to use certain skills, the companionship of a group of people and relationships made with customers. Or it could be the opposite of some of these things: the fact that one does not have to make decisions, or that the person does not have to mix with other people. Both the company and the individual might feel that in return for the benefits the employee would give loyalty to the company, put in extra time during a crisis, and apply skills and abilities beyond the confines of the job description.

When something valued in the psychological contract is taken away, there can be feelings of resentment and resistance. This often happens when organizations change structure or procedures. Take the example of a company that operates on a decentralized, multi-country basis. All local managing directors are responsible for their operations' profitability, and have a high degree of freedom in setting their own policies and strategies. The company decides to take a more centralized approach to its worldwide marketing, which means that product and promotional decisions are taken at the centre. Local factories are no longer treated as part of the local responsibility, but are used as an overall resource, and the managing directors are no longer responsible for them. Job titles are unchanged, and salaries are not affected: indeed, some can earn more because of a new incentive scheme.

The people instigating the change may not understand that the managing directors might feel that they have lost parts of the job that they particularly valued. The psychological contract has been breached, and the job will no longer have the appeal of the past. Therefore, the change may be resisted, and even after it is implemented there may be a form of guerrilla warfare preventing speedy implementation.

Psychological contracts are also formed outside work, with family or bodies, such as the church or a sports club with which an individual may have a particularly deep relationship. A change in what happens at work can cause the individual to fail to fulfil the contract with others. Objections to a change in working hours can, for example, be founded on more than a loss of personal convenience, and cause great concern because one of the other contracts can no longer be kept.

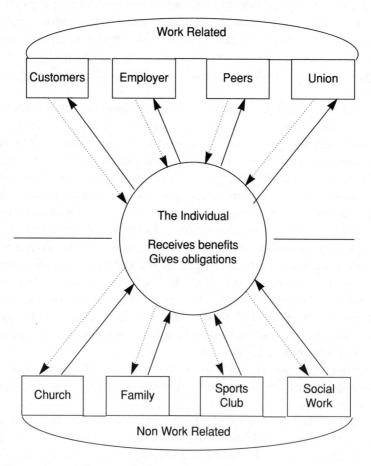

Figure 2.1 *The psychological contract*

Figure 2.1 illustrates this concept. Each pair of arrows represents a psychological contract in either a work related or non-work context. The dotted lines represent benefits obtained, and the solid lines are obligations in return. The various contracting groups are, of course, indicative. For some people their church (used in the sense of any religious group, and not just a building) may be a vital component of their lives: others are indifferent. Some people do not have a family, while others who have faced divorce may have a current partner and a relationship with the children of a previous partner. Some think unpaid social work with charities is not for them: others may believe it to be more worthwhile than anything they ever do at work. Sadly, it is sometimes only the non-work activities that make work bearable.

The above has already indicated that there is a double problem with any changes that affect the psychological contract. Firstly, people may resist a change in the contract because it removes some of the benefits they obtain from the work relationship. Secondly, they may resist a change in the formal contract because it makes it impossible for them to continue an important psychological contract they have outside of work.

However, it is really more difficult than the analysis so far suggests. As the psychological contract with the employer is unwritten, it is not readily apparent what it is, and even the individual may not have consciously thought about it until it comes under threat. The non-work situation is even more obscure, except possibly to colleagues who know each other well. In both situations it may take considerable effort to uncover the critical aspects of the psychological contract. The key that can unlock the hidden doors is trustful communication, and the knowledge that good managers develop through regular contact with their people.

example: changes in the National Health Service

The NHS began a massive change process during the Margaret Thatcher years. Among the changes was a more market-oriented approach, the strengthening of the role of management, and the introduction of more performance targets. More emphasis has been placed on achieving financial results.

One result has been a shift of power from medical staff to a new breed of managers, leading to a belief in some quarters that costs affect patient decisions more than clinical judgement. Nursing is now about economic performance, as well as patient care.

In some areas, the changes have included reductions in hospital beds and the closure of hospitals, but even before this and in areas where closures have not happened, there was considerable resistance from employees within the NHS.

The concept of the psychological contract helps to explain why. Although job titles and salaries may not have changed, and the hours junior doctors are compelled to work are just as penal as they always were, the way things are done is different. Many doctors feel that they have lost some of their rights to exercise clinical judgement, which alters the satisfaction they derive from the job. This may also make them feel that they can no longer as easily fulfil what they may see as their contract with the profession and society as a whole. Nurses frequently join because of compassion and a sense of vocation, and additional issues of management may be seen to be diversions from what they consider to be truly important.

The change of government brought further changes to processes, priorities and jobs. One of the 1999 themes of the Prime Minister has been the 'culture of excuses' that resists change in the whole of the public sector. However, one wonders whether any government, whatever its political persuasion, really understands that there may be more to a reluctance to change than obtuseness and bloody mindedness. There is very often a logic behind the resistance that could have been dealt with up front, if only it had been understood.

your psychological contract

As an exercise in self-understanding, write down the key things you value about your job – not the salary, but the areas that are not part of a formal contract. These might include areas such as being empowered; opportunities to innovate; being respected as an expert; the quality of your peers; the sense of comfort given by the way your office is arranged; the respect of your colleagues; and so forth.

Next, think how you would feel if a change in the organization permanently removed these things. For example, if:

- you now had to get approval before you could implement a decision;
- the new culture of the company meant that innovation could no longer take place;
- your particular expertise was sidelined, and no one thought it critical to the organization or cared about your views;
- your peers had changed and you felt you could not respect the abilities of the replacements;
- someone else rearranged your office in the way they thought was best; your colleagues showed that they had little respect for you...

If you are implementing a change, think about how those changes impinge on the things that those affected might value. If you are involved in something as big as the NHS changes, you can only think about people as groups, but each of those groups has a hierarchy of managers who it is possible to work through. If the number involved is smaller, such as the reorganization of a unit of up to about 100 people, you should be able to think at the individual level. What is the change doing that could impact on the psychological contract of those individuals?

Remember that the question is not whether you would be concerned if you were doing that job, but whether those individuals are likely to be concerned.

---

example: British schools

Another public sector area that has been undergoing almost continuous change over the past decade or more is education at primary and secondary schools. Although there have been changes in political philosophy as a result of changes of government, it is possible to see a continuum of change in terms of more central control over the curricula, centrally determined targets, and a mix of sticks with illusory carrots to drive changes among school heads and teachers. It is almost possible to guarantee that, whenever you read this book and if you live in the UK, you will recently have seen references in the media to objections to many changes by the professions involved and new targets devised by government. Often there are accusations by the profession of the government's lack of understanding of teaching, and by politicians of a culture in the profession that resists anything new. This has been a regular pattern over the past decade, and there is no evidence to suggest that it will be different over the next 10 years. Think over what might be the real causes of resistance, in the light of the continual alterations teachers have had to face in terms of both the formal and psychological contracts. Would thinking this through in advance have affected the way you might have handled these changes if you had been responsible for their implementation? The changes that have been taking place in education have been fundamental, although by no means at crisis level. The approach to change management to the outsider appears to have been dictatorial. In the light of the discussion in the previous chapter and above, do you feel that this has been the most appropriate way to proceed, given the vast numbers of people in the teaching profession? Would it have been possible to take actions to reduce the level of resistance during the time the change strategy was being formulated?

other causes of resistance

While the psychological contract may help us to explain some of the resistance to change that is not immediately obvious, there are other causes. The reason for considering them is to improve understanding (and thereby our ability to forecast the likely response of people to change situations), and to develop ways of reducing resistance. Sometimes it is possible to modify the detail of the change so that some of the causes of resistance are removed, but we should not pretend that this is always possible.

actual threats

Things that are perceived as affecting personal standing or prestige, or as altering the things we value about our jobs, may be real threats although they are intangible and matters of the mind. Some incremental change and most fundamental change is accompanied by job losses, increased workloads for the survivors, and the fear that there will be more job losses later. When an organization like BP or British Telecom talks about a culture change, or GE says it has to be 'lean and agile', or Marks and Spencer says that its cost structure has to be brought in line with its market performance, those inside the company concerned know that there will be casualties as well as survivors. The fear of this type of change, however important that change may be for the future of the organization, or the competitiveness of the country, is justified for many of those who believe they will be affected.

The perceived threat is not always the loss of employment. It may be fear that a lifetime's investment in building up skills and abilities has led to an abyss, and that none of these things will help the person to cope, after the change.

imposed change

For most people change at work has been imposed on them and is not something they have chosen to undergo. The reasons for the change may be unclear, and even in situations where the people will benefit from the change this may be hard to see. Often this means that the vision that those making the change are working to is not shared by those who are affected by the change. You may be totally clear about the soundness of a change you are driving through, but is everybody else? If they do not share your clarity of vision, why is this?

lack of faith in those making the change

Resistance will increase when those in the organization have little respect for the abilities of those who are causing the change. The cynical response of the battle-hardened is often that everything will change back in a month or two, so keep your head down and it might go away. Lack of faith in the management implies that there has been a failure of leadership and, as we will see later, complex change calls for high leadership ability.

a belief that something has been overlooked

People may not be opposed to change itself, but because of their own insight or area of expertise might believe that important aspects have been overlooked, and that the change will cause damage. The 'technical' objections may be well founded or they may be illusory. The planning of change is often weak, and things are overlooked, as in the CSA example. Sometimes, the concerns are a form of rationalization for objecting to the change. In both the NHS and Education change situations there are many genuinely felt technical objections to the things being done, but it would take other experts to sort out which are valid points and which are objections from people who have other reasons for disliking the change.

the head and the heart

In some cases people appear to agree to a course of action because the argument for it is so powerful that they can think of no reason not to agree. However, what the mind accepts and what the emotions cause the person to do may be quite different. Sentiment, loyalty, and the desire for continuity with the past can all bring a resistance to change even when there appears to be an agreement with it.

---

example: aligning the head and the heart

In a major reappraisal of strategy in one of the large UK engineering groups, considerable care was paid to involving the managing directors of the four major groups of business units and the other executive directors in the analysis. A workshop was arranged to enable full discussion of the implications, and for decisions to be reached collectively on the strategy for the whole group. It was clear that the organization did not have the financial resources to support and develop the 60 or so businesses, and that the businesses themselves were in positions of varying strategic importance to the group.

At the workshop there was considerable argument, but eventually a unanimous decision was reached about which businesses should be developed, and which should be sold. The balance of power between the top team was largely undisturbed. It was agreed that the managing directors of the business units targeted for disposal should be advised that the outline strategy would be shared with all heads of business units. It was also agreed that the divisional managing directors to whom the businesses reported would set in hand the actions to sell the unwanted businesses.

One year later very little had happened, apart from the fact that the full board had approved the strategy shortly after the workshop. The reasons for the lack of action on a strategy with which there was full intellectual agreement were emotional. For example, one of the group managing directors had built his reputation in earlier times by turning round a business that had been in a parlous state. This business was one that it had been agreed should be sold. For him it was like saying that his past achievement was no longer important, and was also a betrayal of the management colleagues still in that unit and with whom he had worked on the turnaround. Others found it difficult to deal at two levels: discussing plans with the management of the businesses at the same time as they were trying to dispose of the business.

The logic of the actions was reaffirmed and all the analysis was re-examined to ensure that nothing had been missed. Then with the agreement of all the executive directors, the responsibility for disposing of businesses was separated from that of management, and this responsibility was given to one of the other directors. Within 12 months most of the businesses had been sold.

Logically, this could have happened a year earlier. It was the heart that prevented the action, not the head.

reducing resistance

In any change situation thought should be given to the potential resistance to the change and to ways of reducing the drag that resistance to change can have on effective implementation.

participation

Participation can help to reduce resistance in many situations. Chapter 1 suggested this as an appropriate approach to change in some situations. It also suggested when focused participation was more appropriate than broad participation. Participation can create ownership of the proposed change, and because it creates a better awareness of the change, and the reasons for it, it can remove uncertainties and enable those involved to identify with the benefits. Working on the change can bring conviction that the actions being taken are correct. The change may be better planned because those with knowledge are involved in it: or it may be thought by them to be better planned because of this involvement.

However, it may not always be appropriate, or even possible, to have a widespread involvement in the change decision. In such a situation much may sometimes be gained if those affected are involved in working out how to implement the change.

---

example: BAT Industries plc

BAT Industries developed a learning method of achieving participation, through the development of a business management seminar for management teams. The process required a director to choose an area of concern to be dealt with in a three-stage process at the seminar.

Stage 1 was a half-day pre-seminar briefing of the director and some six or seven of the people reporting to that director, during which the process would be described and the types of information that needed to be brought to the next stage discussed. Stage 2 came a month later, when the same people would attend a six-day seminar to develop solutions to the issue, with action plans that included exploration of the organizational behavioural implications. Over the six days there were also inputs from the faculty and tutorial team, to help the participants develop an understanding of the implications of the changes they were working through. Stage 3 came some eight months after this seminar, when a four-day follow-up progress meeting was held. This consisted of the original group, plus a number of others who were found to be important in implementing the plans. This meeting re-examined the strategy, reviewed progress, and developed new

action plans where necessary. It also had the support from a
faculty experienced in change management.

In this example participation was focused, and was about
creating individual and organizational learning, as well as
bringing about change.

Points to consider when thinking about participation include:

- ■ Is participation desirable in the circumstances? Why?
  Why not?
- ■ Are there circumstances that prevent participation?
  Can they be removed?
- ■ Who should participate: key people; your direct
  reports; everybody concerned?
- ■ What is the scope for participation: decision making;
  post-decision implementation?
- ■ How should participation be achieved: individual dis-
  cussions with each person; group meetings; working
  parties?

communication

In all change situations good communication can help to
reduce resistance by ensuring that the reasons for the change
are clear, the degree of urgency is understood and that all
concerned know what the change means. Resistance may be
lowered in a crisis if the people know there is a crisis.

Points that should be considered in planning communication
include:

- ■ Who are the target groups who should receive the
  communication?
- ■ What should be communicated?

■ What mix of one-way and two-way communication should be planned?

■ What style of communication should be used: should this be the same for all groups?

■ Does the message being communicated address the concerns that those affected by the change are likely to feel?

■ What mode of communication should be used?

---

example: British Petroleum project 1990

Communication played a key part in the major changes initiated by BP under the Project 1990 initiative. Among the numerous methods used were some that were unusual. A senior journalist from the *Financial Times* was invited to the board meetings, which reviewed the need for fundamental change, and wrote a series of articles describing what happened. Carefully composed documents about the nature of the change and the reasons for it were widely distributed. Widespread meetings were held at various levels to begin the change process, which both communicated and began a process of participation in implementation.

(Note: more detail on the BP case appears on pages 61–62.)

---

training

Training is rarely considered as a means of reducing resistance to change, because too few organizations consider what new requirements of skills, knowledge and abilities are being created by the change. For example, in the prevalent delayering actions taken by organizations there is often talk of empowering those closest to the customer, yet very few of those organizations have taken steps to ensure that the newly empowered people and their managers understand and can apply the skills needed to work in the new manner. We have already seen that fear of being unable to cope with a new situation may be one reason for resistance. A training approach designed specifically to help the implementation of the change can also serve as a means of communication and provide a measure of participation.

Points to consider for both incremental and fundamental change are:

- How different will the job of each person be after the change, in terms of content and style?
- Do their skills, knowledge and abilities match these requirements?
- How confident are the people concerned that they know and understand the new requirements, and possess the required competencies?
- Would a training initiative provide a mechanism to enable wider participation in the change process or, as a minimum, enable concerns to be expressed and dealt with?

---

example: how training can reduce resistance

A leading toiletries company undertook careful analysis of its market position, with a view to developing a strategy to increase its market share. Although its overall share in its product categories was only just in double figures, it had a disproportionately high share of the business passing through certain retail organizations such as Boots. The conclusion was that it would not be possible to increase share by concentrating on those outlets where success was already very high, and that increases had to come from improving distribution in other types of outlet. Currently the sales force was not organized to reach many of these outlets, and merchandising was separate from selling.

Success lay in combining the sales and merchandising teams, and reorganizing the sales activity so that it encompassed all the target outlet types. This would mean that all representatives would be required to operate in a different way, and to deal with outlets that were new to them. The new structure was designed and announced, and at the same time a series of seminars was planned to ensure that all concerned understood the reasons for the change, and were confident that they possessed the competencies needed to operate in the new way.

The seminars began with a case study that used real market data but required an expansion strategy to be developed for a fictitious company that was very similar to the real organization. This gave the whole sales force an opportunity to explore whether there were other ways of achieving the objectives and understanding the reasoning behind the changes. They had not previously had any detailed analysis of the strategic situation. All the small groups, over four repeats of the seminar, concluded that the only way forward would be to widen the base of distribution.

A training input built an understanding of the requirements of the new outlets they would be approaching, and included participation by customers. Skills needed to meet the new requirements were built into the programme. The new structure was explained again, in relation to the conclusions the participants had reached. Final sessions enabled the participants to examine their own concerns, and identify needs that had not been met by the seminar.

The seminar organizers were concerned that participation, in the limited way it was used in this initiative, should not become manipulation. For this reason they insisted that the structural changes were announced before people attended the seminars. The correctness of this decision became apparent during the final seminar, when one participant exploded with anger when he saw the pre-printed organograms halfway through the seminar. He felt that he was the victim of a confidence trick to make him feel that he was helping to determine the company response, when in fact all the decisions had been taken already. He soon realized that it was only he who had not seen the charts before as he had missed the pre-seminar briefing session on the new structure. He had been on leave at the time, and the regional manager had overlooked the fact that he had been away. However, the incident shows the need to plan such initiatives as this very carefully.

The company announced after a year that the seminars had been the major factor in helping them to achieve the new market share targets, and in addition had reduced the normal turnover of sales people. In this example, the training did three things:

■ it built an understanding of the need for change, and moved from understanding to creating a commitment to the new approach;
■ it communicated the changes in an effective way;
■ it helped to build confidence in each individual's ability to cope with new requirements, and provided help in areas of weakness.

thinking about attitude change

Common sense and your own experience will allow you to see the validity of much of what has been said so far about reducing resistance. Many of the causes of resistance, and the remedies, are related to attitudes and values of the individuals affected. We should not pretend that every cause of resistance is just a question of attitude change: a well-founded fear of redundancy will, for most people, be somewhat more fundamental. But there are many changes, where things would work better if attitudes could be changed. Examples are the major attempts to change corporate culture that some organizations have undergone, changes in systems and procedures, such as a new computer system, or a different approach to manufacturing, or changes in structure and the expectations of individuals.

Figure 2.2 is a simplified view of two determinants that lie behind the acceptance or rejection of some types of change. It implies that individuals have values and attitudes and that both of these have an effect on behaviour. It should not be read to imply that these are the only variables that matter, and we have already examined a few different causes:

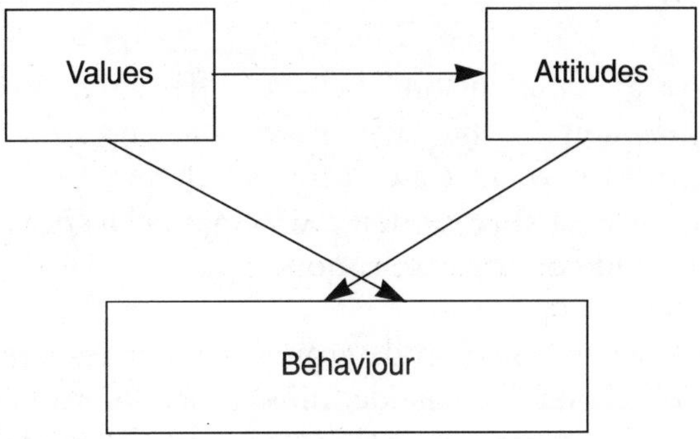

Figure 2.2 *Values and attitudes*

■ Values are strongly held beliefs that are fundamental to the person. They may have developed over many years, and have been influenced by family upbringing, peer groups, and affiliations with religious, professional and other social groups. At their most fundamental, they determine beliefs about right and wrong. They may be based on perceptions rather than reality. Values do change over time, but it is by no means a simple and quick task for an organization to set about changing the fundamental values of its employees.

■ Attitudes are more transient. Some may derive from values, but others may be based on perceptions, knowledge, or even ignorance. The advertising industry is always trying to manipulate our attitudes. Not all attitudes may be deeply held: they may condition behaviour today, but something may happen to change minds in the future. We may have felt in 1999 that we should stop buying French apples because of France's 'unfair' refusal to lift the ban on beef from the UK, but this does not mean that we would all be thinking badly of France three months later.

■ Behaviour is what we do. It is shaped by our values and our attitudes, and because we are individuals we are all different and behave differently. Where there are many people who share widespread values and attitudes we have a culture, which may be national, or a much smaller grouping within a profession, religious movement, or organization.

When we involve others in determining what response should be made once someone has identified a need for a change, we are using participation to help shape new attitudes and to modify others that might otherwise have been opposed to the actions. Similarly, the communication strategy might be trying to share knowledge of a situation, so that favourable attitudes may develop as a response to it.

However, we should not expect that a change in attitude will always automatically bring about a change in behaviour. For example, someone could develop an anti-smoking attitude, but continue to smoke out of habit or addiction.

It is also sometimes possible to change or shape attitudes by getting people to behave differently, so that the results they experience are what takes them to a new attitude. This is partly what happens when we ask people to participate in working out and implementing a predetermined change, or to participate in a training event that will give them a chance to experience the new situation and explore how it will affect them. By working on the new situation, it is possible for those once opposed to it to become convinced of its value.

But remember that human behaviour is very complex. Badly implemented participation may be seen as a confidence trick and can make matters worse. Dictatorially driven behaviour may set up waves of resentment and prevent favourable attitudes to the change from being developed. Personal fears and concerns may create a state of mind that overshadows an individual's interpretation of every action by management.

example: an extreme case of resistance to change
Fortunately comparatively few change situations result in the type
of action that occurred when the three top security mental health
hospitals in the UK were transferred from the Prison Service to the
National Health Service. In May 1997 *The Times* reported that
about 150 members of the Prisons Officers Association were
waging a war against the managers and nurses who had joined
from the NHS. The resistance was partly due to a loss of negoti-
ating rights by the POA, and partly because of disagreement with
the more caring attitude to patients of the NHS nurses.

Resistance took the form of hate mail and verbal abuse directed
at managers and the NHS colleagues, threatening physical
behaviour, and putting a toy hand grenade under the car of one
of the senior managers.

responses of implementers of change

Figure 2.3 is derived from some ideas by Larry Alexander (see
page 86 for more on Larry Alexander's views on implementation), although the descriptions of each box in the matrix have
been changed. They refer to the actions of the key implementers of a change. One dimension shows the implementer's
agreement with the change; the other shows the degree of effort
applied by the implementer to effecting the change.

pretender

Pretenders agree with the strategy but do not put in more than
a token effort to make it work – they pretend to be working on
it. The reasons may be lack of time to do what should be done,
a perception that the change will have an adverse effect on the
implementer personally (as in the hearts and minds example),

EFFORT BY KEY IMPLEMENTER
TO IMPLEMENT

	LOW	HIGH
HIGH IMPLEMENTER'S AGREEMENT WITH CHANGE	PRETENDER	LEADER
LOW	DISSENTER	FOLLOWER

Figure 2.3 *Responses of implementers of change*

This diagram was stimulated by concepts developed by L Alexander in 'Strategy implementation: the nature of the problem', in D E Hussey (editor), *International Review of Strategic Management*, **2**(1), John Wiley & Sons, Chichester, 1991.

or the reward system drives the implementer towards actions. The danger is that only some of the steps for successful implementation will be taken, but because there is agreement about the appropriateness of the change this may go undetected for some time.

dissenter

The dissenter may actively work against successful implementation, at worst sabotaging the change, and at best doing nothing to implement it. Dissent may arise from a certainty that 'they' have got it wrong, a belief that time should be directed to more important areas, or total resentment that the change will have personal disadvantages. Unfortunately, many dissenters work in secret, and either do not voice their opposition when given the opportunity, or are never given the chance to do so.

leader

Here we have the implementer who believes in the change and puts in considerable effort to ensure its successful implementation. Usually, such people will apply some of the concepts of transformational leadership to motivate others to aid the change process.

follower

Typically, these people do many of the right things because they have faith in their leader, rather than any particular faith in the change itself. 'If the boss thinks it's right, that's good enough for me.' Also in this box are those who see the change as less important than their career in the organization. They therefore do their best to make the change work because they want to be seen to be making the change work. The danger is that they may not see the less obvious things that need to be done, such as retraining.

understanding the change

the need

Effective change management requires attention to detail, and planning comes in at two places. The first, which is the subject of this chapter, is to think through all aspects of the implications of the change. The second, which we will meet later, is to set out all the actions that need to take place in order to ensure that the change is implemented.

Chapter 2 began this process, when we looked at the possible causes of resistance, and suggested trying to anticipate where these might occur so that actions could be taken to reduce or remove the resistance where this was possible.

Chapter 1 provided an example of the CSA, where neither the implications of the change nor its implementation appeared to have been fully thought through. The need for forethought applies to both incremental and fundamental change, and the approach of this chapter applies to both, although some of the specific methods may be of more value to one type of change than the other.

Arguing that change should be thought through may seem to

be stating the obvious. Unfortunately, it needs to be stated. An example will make the point. In 1973, Kitching researched the failure rates of acquisitions in Europe, and reached the conclusion that 53 per cent can be considered failures. In 1987 Porter studied US acquisitions and found a failure rate of 50 per cent. In 1993 Coopers & Lybrand published a study in the UK and found a failure rate of 50 per cent. Now guess what failure rate consultants A T Kearney found in their recent study! It seems that over this whole period little has been learnt about ensuring success with this particular strategic change. Although study after study has shown that success is very dependent on what happens to implement an acquisition after the deal is concluded, study after study also shows that too many organizations pay inadequate attention to this. A 1997 study of British acquisitions by Warwick Business School concluded that so much management energy was used in closing the deal that none was left for the post-purchase implementation. A KPMG European study carried out in 1997 found that many implications of a proposed acquisition were left late in the process. The study report stated:

> Timescales are not properly assessed. Strategies for different facets of the transaction, such as culture, human resources and information technology, are left too far down the line, especially in the case of IT.

The point is that the failure rate would be considerably reduced if more of the implications of the acquisition were understood before the change in ownership instead of emerging afterwards. The implications can affect both the buying and selling organizations: when two organizations are crashed together, employees in both may face uncertainty and the possibility of losing their jobs.

The point made in some detail here can be extended to all major change situations. For example, a reduction in the scale of an organization is not implemented when people are made redundant and have left: the real effort is making the new organization operationally effective.

Understanding the implications of the change may some-times give an indication that the proposed change is misguided. It may lead to a different implementation strategy, and will almost always show that there are many aspects of the change that must not be neglected.

So let's look at some tools that can help us understand the implications of a change. But let us not overlook that although the tools may help us to be systematic, we are likely to use them more wisely if there is an addition of sound common sense and a good knowledge of the organization.

force field analysis

Force field analysis was developed by Kurt Lewin, and it provides a very useful way of looking at a problem. The partic-ular approach described here has been used in a number of change situations and is suitable for individual use by the manager planning the change, or as a means of stimulating thinking in a small group of people. Its strength is that the tech-nique requires only the skill to draw a few straight lines on a flip chart and the ability to harness the knowledge of people who understand the issue.

Every situation has forces at work on it. If we think of an organization's market share, we can visualize a number of forces that keep the share as high as it is, and a number that press down on it and keep it as low as it is. Things that hold it up might include the product, good distribution and the image of the product. Things that hold it down might include competitor advertising, our own poor customer relations, and factory delivery problems.

Figure 3.1 visualizes this in a simple diagram. The horizontal line represents the current market share. The downward pointing arrows show the three forces we identified pushing down on our share and preventing it from rising. The three positive forces are the upward pointing arrows. The scale at the side is a simple way of trying to assess the relative importance of each arrow. It has no great mathematical significance, and one reason why you should not worry if the scores do not add up to an equal number at the top and bottom of the diagram is that only rarely will we be clever enough to identify all the factors. However, the idea is clear: some of the downward forces are pressing harder than others, because they have extra weightings on them; some of the upward forces can be seen thrust forward by springs, which exert varying pressures.

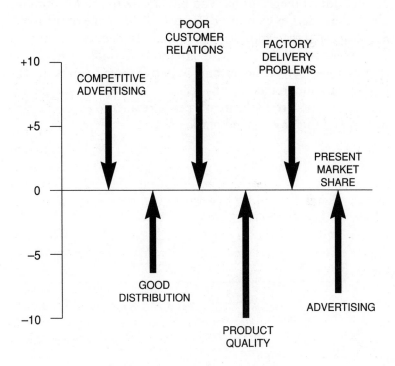

Figure 3.1 *Force field (or equilibrium) analysis*

In our example, we can try to increase our market share by attacking the bottom part of the diagram and reinforcing the things that hold the share up (for example, increasing advertising to negate the effect of the competitors'). Or we can remove some of the things that hold us down, and in this example we might achieve more by addressing the two negatives that are internal to us: the poor customer relations and our own delivery problems.

This illustration is only to show how the approach works, and the market share example was chosen for simplicity. Figure 3.2 provides a diagram that you might care to use for thinking about the toiletries example on pages 40–42. Some of the issues are clear from the example; others might be deduced from your own experience of this sort of situation. We look at the situation as it was before the training initiative was undertaken. The horizontal line refers to the change needed to enable the company to penetrate the new types of retailer to expand distribution and thereby expand market share.

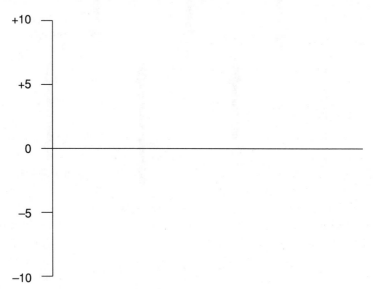

Figure 3.2   *Use this to analyse the toiletries example*

In my analysis of this situation I have restricted myself to the behavioural issues that influence the success or failure of the change. I have not used the approach to examine the strategy behind the change, although this would be a sensible thing to do. My suggestions are:

downward pressures

- Lack of understanding of the new strategy by sales representatives.
- Unwillingness of sales people to undertake the new tasks.
- Lack of competence of sales force in the new areas.
- The reward systems stress the old strategy.
- High turnover of sales representatives.
- No relationships with the new customers.
- No understanding of the needs of these retailers.
- Old organization structure does not match strategy.

upward pressures

- Customer service philosophy of sales force.
- Drive from top management.
- Sales force wants the company to grow.

The new structure, and the training approach to help make it work, addressed many of these downward pressures, and should have removed many of them. In fact, the exciting thing about behavioural issues is that in many situations we gain more than simply removing a negative: it also creates a new upward pressure. At the end of the training initiative the organization had strong support from the sales force, creating a positive force for success. If we were really part of the toiletries situation we would no doubt be aware of other pressures in both directions, and we would have an understanding of the weightings of the various pressures. I slipped in a possible downward pressure that could not have been read from the information given, reward systems being out of step with the new requirements. This was deliberate, as it will provide a lead into the next section where another model is offered to help think through the implications of change.

A benefit of the force field or equilibrium analysis is that it helps us think of more of the pressures that might otherwise impede our desired change. It helps us to see which ones are likely to be the most critical for our success, and also which are likely to be the easiest to deal with. The analysis should lead us to think of actions in our change implementation programme that might otherwise have escaped us. The main value of the approach is to help us decide what should be done to overcome the issues, or in extreme cases to decide that the change is totally unworkable and therefore to be avoided.

The advantage of having a number of people involved in the exercise is that important implications are more likely to be spotted. Few managers can have an intimate knowledge of every issue in their areas of responsibility. In the example above, top management may not have known of the concerns of members of the sales force that they did not have the competencies needed for quick success after the change. Involvement in the thinking process of someone closer to the sales force might have alerted them to this. Our example is from a company that did recognize the issues. Unfortunately, many change situations are not as well thought out.

the integrated organization

Change can be frustrated because different drivers in the organization are pushing people in different directions, and in these situations the strongest wins. An intention to emphasize teamwork could, for example, be frustrated if the rewards in terms of merit increases and promotions only emphasized individual performance. It is no good telling a sales force to sell high-margin products if commission is based on sales volume and they can achieve higher volumes from low-margin products. The toiletries example was a situation where the new market share targets would have been impossible to achieve without the accompanying changes in both tasks and structure.

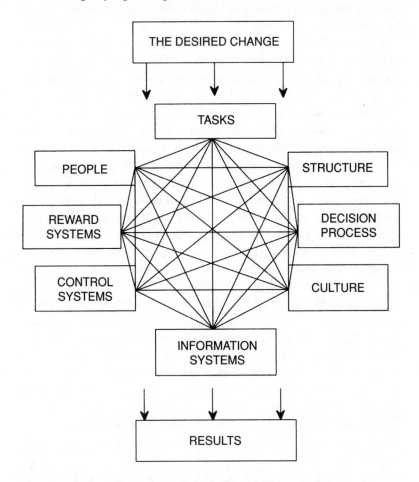

Figure 3.3 *The integrated organization*

(A modified version of a diagram in *Strategic Management Theory and Practice*, D E Hussey, Butterworth Heinemann, 1994)

Figure 3.3 provides one way of thinking about those integrated aspects of the organization that have to pull in the same direction if change is to be effective. The important point is that changes in any one factor in the octagon can affect performance in all or any of the others. Change will not be implemented in an effective way unless all eight factors are in harmony.

The model should be driven by the strategy, which for most purposes may be defined as the actions the organization intends to take in order to achieve its aims. We can use the word 'strategy' at every level in the organization, and can apply it to the change a manager is trying to implement. The desired output from the model is results: the achievement of the purpose for which the strategy was designed.

What the organization wishes to be done requires people to perform certain tasks. These tasks are affected by technology. We have had accountants for several hundred years, but personal computers only began to be widely used in the 1980s, and did not become commonplace until the last decade. Now there can be few accountants whose tasks have not changed because they now have access to PCs. Tasks are also affected by the manner in which the strategy requires them to be performed. A simple example is the manner in which announcements are made at railway stations. For many years British Rail apologized to passengers for a late train. Then the word 'passenger' appeared to have been banned and we were all 'customers'. Presumably this was an attempt to undertake all tasks in a customer-responsive way, although for most of us this was the only noticeable change. I usually see myself as a victim, not a customer, a view that has not changed with the disappearance of British Rail and its replacement by private companies.

Tasks are influenced by people: by their experience, competencies, attitudes and availability. In some change situations it is possible to train people to fulfil the new requirements, but in others it may be necessary to recruit new people with the required skills. In a downsizing situation the problem may be too many people for the new situation. On the other hand, an expansion strategy may be delayed or frustrated because of difficulty in obtaining people with the competencies needed. People do not have to be employees to be considered under this heading, as it is possible to use outsourcing or consultants to fill some of the needs. The skills of people affect how tasks are drawn together to make jobs.

The structure is the way jobs are grouped into units for management and control purposes, and the various levels of management that are deemed to be needed. In the toiletries case, the existing structure had to be changed because it prevented the sales force from dealing with the new types of outlet. A rigid multi-layered structure may be great if the organization is in a stable business environment and there is a need to ensure that every person does precisely what he or she is told. The same structure may stifle initiative and may be totally inappropriate if the strategy changes in order to meet the challenges of a more turbulent outside world.

What makes a structure work is something more than the people. It is the way the processes and systems in the organization operate. Decision processes are about how power is distributed and exercised. They reflect the style of the organization and the depth and nature of empowerment throughout the organization. The airline SAS changed its decision processes in the 1980s to empower those dealing with a customer to take decisions that affected that customer. This altered the role of middle management and caused change to both the structure and some of the people.

Information systems affect the ability of managers to make good decisions and to manage their units. If the flow of information is not adjusted to a change in structure, the new structure may become unworkable. The nature of information required may also change as strategy changes.

Control systems relate closely to decision processes and affect behaviour. The way the budget system works, for example, could drive managers to take actions that are not compatible with the desired change. If a change requires some capital expenditure as well as expense, and the system will release only the expense, it is likely that the change will be frustrated. Necessary training might not be provided because there is no provision for it in the budget, despite the fact that this will frustrate the change.

Reward systems have been discussed earlier. It is usually a fair assumption that people will do what the reward and control systems indicate the organization really wants rather than follow the exhortations of managers, even when they agree with what the manager is asking them to do.

The final element of the model is culture. This is influenced by the way the decision, control and reward processes work, plus some very important additional factors. The latter include:

■ the style and values of top management;
■ the history and evolution of the organization;
■ the business of the organization;
■ the speed of change in the business environment and the nature of those changes.

After the disastrous Paddington rail crash in 1999, the environment and transport minister, John Prescott, argued that changes needed to be made in the railway companies from a culture of blame to a culture of safety. Whether he was right in this diagnosis is not known, but it is clear that desirable changes to safety measures could be frustrated if the culture and processes in an organization were to always put profit first when making safety decisions. It is also possible to see that the way the privatized railway industry was set up by the previous government could lead to certain aspects of culture. As the procedure for compensation to the train operators from Railtrack for delays to service depends on determining who was to blame, it is not hard to imagine that the systems would drive management behaviour and that this behaviour would in turn affect culture.

How decision processes work in the organization is both an effect of the culture and a way in which the culture is shaped within the organization. There are a large number of causes that become effects, and effects that become causes. The strongest influence on culture is top management, and this is reinforced by the way each manager in the organization performs the task of management. There are differences in culture between different parts of any organization, but these are normally linked by some all-pervading shared values. Below top management it is very difficult for anyone to change the culture, partly because the rebels tend to be forced out of the organization, and partly because so many of the other elements in Figure 3.3 drive behaviour so that it fits the culture. Usually, new people gradually adapt to the culture of the organization or leave early because they feel uncomfortable.

Many incremental changes require little attention to the organizational model, because the changes are within the context of the current organization. However, this is not true of all incremental change: the toiletries example is of an incremental change that impacted on several of the factors of the model. Fundamental change is likely to have an even greater impact on the factors. In some cases a fundamental change may require major changes to every factor in the model, and this of course is often why such changes may be difficult to implement effectively.

One complication, which we have already seen, is that each factor in the model is an umbrella description, which means that there may be many sub-factors to investigate.

Another complication, not quite so obvious, is that there may be many strategies in the organization, and factors that support some of these may hinder others. Thus a sales bonus system may be ideal for most of the products the organization offers, but not for the new product you are expected to introduce. This can make changes more difficult, and more complex to assess, unless the changes you need to make can be isolated from the organization at large. So identifying what needs to be done, and getting agreement to do it, may take more of an effort than a brief description of the model has suggested.

The implications of the model when a change situation is faced are:

■ Does each factor shown in the model contribute to the implementation of the change?

■ If not, which sub-factors require attention in order to enable the change to be effective?

■ If any factors require change, how will this affect the other factors in the model, bearing in mind the integrated nature of the model?

■ Do the changes needed to any sub-factor have an impact on other areas of the organization?

■ Is it possible for the person managing the particular change situation to bring about the modifications to the sub-factors that are necessary?

■ If it is not possible, should the proposed change be abandoned or approached in a different way?

■ If it is possible, what actions have to be taken to bring about the organizational change that will be part of the change strategy?

It is not easy to attune the organization so that it enables the new situation to be implemented, partly because the integrated nature of the factors makes it difficult to make anything but the smallest of piecemeal changes to any one factor. Solve a structural problem without attention to the other factors and all that happens is that a new problem is created. There are also many hidden elements. For example, a chief executive may have produced a culture statement that states that decisions will be delegated to the lowest possible level in the organization, but his or her own behaviour makes this impossible. So what is said and what happens are two very different things.

Many of the high-profile fundamental changes have taken culture as the key change element. This is rarely a matter of whimsy, and is a response to both the current strategic situation of the organization and the way that situation is expected to evolve in the future. However, there are probably no situations where culture can be changed in isolation from the other factors in the organizational model.

---

example: British Petroleum again

A few details were given about the change strategy of BP in the preceding chapter. The following case history is quoted from my book *Strategic Management: From Theory to Implementation* (see further reading) and gives at least a flavour of the complexity facing any organization that seeks to change culture.

It is not possible to have a higher profile in a change process than to invite a journalist to sit in and write about the board meetings where the change strategy is decided.

BP's change strategy was the result of a very detailed analysis involving many people. In July 1989, the chairman designate, Robert Horton, commissioned Project 1990, a major internal study that had the aim of showing how to reduce complexity in the organization, to redesign the head office organization, and to reposition the company in approach and style for the 1990s. The project team consulted widely inside and outside of BP, undertaking over 500 interviews and processing some 4,000 questionnaires.

The implementation of the culture change began in 1990, when Horton was appointed chairman. Its objective was to achieve the BP vision through the people, within a simple, supportive organization. The process followed a number of principles:

- ■ The need for change was analysed in a way that took information from many people, as described above.
- ■ Considerable effort was given to inspiring enthusiasm for change, involving communication of various types, and including explanations of the need for change.

> ■ The emphasis was on building an organization for the future, and the structure chosen was unusual enough to be exciting.
>
> ■ Top management drove the change process and provided adequate resources for implementation.
>
> ■ There was widespread involvement of everyone in the change process, including a major educational initiative.
>
> ■ Processes were developed to support the change, including the identification of the competencies needed for employees working under the new culture.
>
> ■ There was continuous review of the change process.
>
> Of course, things did not always go smoothly, and a major problem was an increase in environmental turbulence at the time the change process started. The UK moved into recession in 1990, and the worldwide oil industry found oil prices declining. This meant that certain strategies for disposing of non-core businesses became more urgent, and more costs had to be taken out of the company. In addition to the planned changes leading to a smaller head office and more putting out of work to third parties, there were other factors that meant that many people had to leave the company.
>
> Change was thus implemented against a background of budgetary pressure, terminations and early retirements. Part way through the process the chief executive left the company. However, the strength of the change process was that culture has changed in the direction desired, despite all the additional complications and individual uncertainties.

If you want any change to happen, you have to ensure that the factors in the integrated model work for the change and not against it. The first step is to gain a complete understanding of the change in relation to each and all of the other factors.

Johari windows

The psychological contract was discussed at some length in the previous chapter, and one of the problems raised was the difficulty of finding out the 'details' of this contract. It was suggested that a key to understanding was trustful communication between a manager and subordinates, and the knowledge that a manager develops when there is a close working relationship with those subordinates. Obviously, knowledge of the psychological contract can never be perfect, but even an understanding of some of the issues can lead to ways of dealing with the change that increase the odds for success. In addition, trustful communication can lead a manager to a much better understanding of the strengths and weaknesses of each person, which may be very helpful when determining the levels of participation and delegation that might take place during a change management situation.

Figure 3.4 presents a way of thinking about interpersonal communication that enables one person to develop trust and increase understanding with another. It is something that ideally should be used in all situations over a long period, and not only when you have to manage a change situation. The concept describes one-on-one communication, so it can only be applied with people with whom you have the opportunity for regular discourse. Most managers have the opportunity for one-to-one discourses with all their direct reports, and a number of peers as well.

The diagram represents you, as the manager, and another person. In any situation there are things that are known to you, and things that are unknown to you. Similarly there are things that the other person knows and things that are unknown to that person. Figure 3.4 shows the four states that result in a matrix, and for ease of presentation assumes that each of the windows is of equal size, which is not the aim. Things that are known to both parties form a window called the arena. Things

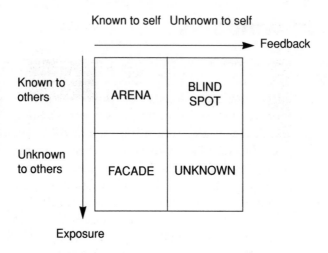

Figure 3.4 *Johari windows*
(named after its originators Joe Lufts and Harry Ingham)

that you know and others do not are in the facade area. There is also a blind spot, which relates to things you do not know, but the other person does, and an unknown area where you are both ignorant.

Figure 3.5 shows one healthy interpersonal communication situation and three that are unhealthy, for various reasons.

Healthy interpersonal communication comes about when the area of common knowledge expands. In this context knowledge has a wide meaning. It may be a fact, information, a feeling, or an opinion. If you have ever watched an episode of the TV series *The Bill*, you may have noticed that frequently part of the drama illustrates the problems when communication is like C) in Figure 3.5. Let us outline a script! Two officers from the Drug Squad have a London-wide operation underway, hoping to catch a drug baron in the act, but have not told the CID branch of the local police station. Meanwhile a CID officer arrests a person who happens to be carrying drugs, in connection with a totally different investigation. By

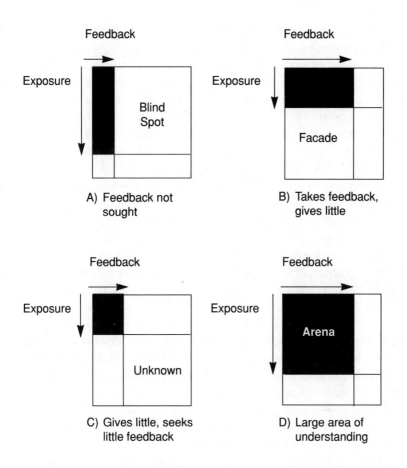

Figure 3.5 *Unhealthy and healthy communication*

chance he is the person under observation, who should have led the Drug Squad to the top crook. Drug Squad are upset. Meanwhile, one of the heroes from uniformed branch has information about where the suspected top crook is living, but does not know that he is involved in any crime so does nothing with it. As the drama unfolds, information is shared and the area of common understanding enlarges. As it is a drama, this usually results in the crook being arrested. In management, in real life, a similar situation may not have a happy ending.

In our *Bill* example we can see that if the Drug Squad officers had exposed their knowledge to the local station, CID would have held back on their arrest and, equally importantly, Drug Squad would have received feedback from the uniformed officer that would have been of considerable value. The combination of all the information had a side-effect of reducing the unknown, thus enabling a problem to be solved. This would have reduced a one-hour TV episode to 10 minutes! Johari windows also work with some of the less obvious matters that are important in a management situation: feelings, opinions, and personal matters that impact on a business situation.

The two elements of the model are exposure (what you share with the other person) and feedback (what you solicit from the other person). Both are equally important. Diagram A) in Figure 3.5 illustrates what happens when you stress exposure at the expense of feedback. We have all met those people who manage to turn every conversation into a discourse about themselves, and allow no change of their favourite subject. At worst this is how you could come across if you were to follow the unbalanced approach illustrated. Certainly, the other person would know a great deal about you (if he or she did not mentally switch off), but you would know very little about them, or any information that they have.

Diagram B) offers the other side of the same coin. Here you are either dealing with someone else whose only interest is themselves, or more likely you as the manager are continually shooting off questions, but are giving nothing in return. So the result is that you amass information, but only if you have asked a direct question. Releasing something from your side might well have prompted more information from the other person, because it would have enlarged the area of relevance in the eyes of that person, or may have brought a realization that you did not know something that he or she did.

The way to expand the arena is to give exposure of your own

knowledge at the same time as you obtain feedback. This does not mean that either party should indulge in a monologue. The idea is both to give and receive information so that the common area, the arena, can expand. It means that you have to be willing to listen, as well as to speak, to encourage feedback from the other person and to give feedback to that person.

Here are a few pointers to help apply this concept:

General

- ■ Do not reserve the method for crisis or change situations: make it part of your management style.
- ■ Do not become unnecessarily secretive when you are in a change situation.
- ■ Remember that to work, interpersonal communication should be genuinely two-way.
- ■ Do not give a meaningless, politician-like answer to a question that you wish to avoid.
- ■ Remember that neither party has a licence to pry into deeply personal affairs. A work relationship does not give anyone the right to try to act as a marriage counsellor, or to force a person to talk about private matters that he or she would prefer to remain hidden.
- ■ Create regular opportunities for discussion, even though many might last only a few minutes.

In relation to exposure

- ■ Be positive.
- ■ Think of what you are revealing in terms of the usefulness to the other person.
- ■ Do not withhold relevant information for other than genuine reasons.
- ■ Ensure that other persons understand what you tell them.
- ■ Use repetition to emphasize key points.
- ■ Do not wander off the subject for no useful purpose.
- ■ Never lie.

- Be willing to listen to criticism without becoming angry.
- Treat people with respect and courtesy.

In relation to feedback: effective questioning

- Use open-ended questions.
- Invite people to expand on what they have said.
- Do not put words into people's mouths.
- Avoid phrasing questions in a way that makes people defensive.
- Do not signal the answer you would like to hear.
- Show genuine interest.
- Make the questioning part of two-way communication.

In relation to feedback: active listening

- Concentrate.
- Do not guess what the person is about to say.
- Do not interrupt, but use verbal signals to encourage.
- Use non-verbal signals to encourage: avoid those that may discourage.
- Seek confirmation that you have understood properly.
- Treat the other person with respect.

Johari windows are about developing a healthy, open communication that allows every one to function better, at the same time avoiding many problems caused by misunderstandings. The by-product is that if you have followed such an approach, you should be able to understand more about the probable effects a change may make to each of your team. This is important information in a change situation, in that it may lead to a modification of the change, or to actions being built into the implementation process that may mitigate the effects. And knowing all this, you will be in a better position to obtain effective participation from those who report directly to you.

leading fundamental change

the EASIER way to lead change

Many writers and researchers have given attention to the issue
of how to lead effective change, particularly the type of change
I have called 'fundamental', but which in many other books has
been termed 'transformational' or 'visionary'. There are, of
course, differences between the various models and concepts
developed, but also many similarities. The approach suggested
puts the essential steps into an approach that I hope will be
EASIER to remember. The acronym stands for:

- Envisioning
- Activating
- Supporting
- Implementing
- Ensuring
- Recognizing.

The main value of this approach is in leading fundamental change. It is also appropriate for major incremental change, and elements of the model can be used for any other change situation. In this chapter the emphasis will be on fundamental change, because it is in this type of situation that the leader has to visualize a completely different situation, and inspire others to help in the re-creation of the organization to achieve this new vision.

The EASIER approach can be seen under two broad headings. The first three elements, envisioning, activating and supporting, are the charismatic and behavioural aspects of leadership. The second three elements, implementing, ensuring and recognizing, are the management and administrative aspects that enable the first three to be converted to effective actions.

An analogy might be drawn with an army, where the soundness of the general's strategy and the inspiration of the officers are key factors in success. However, success cannot occur unless adequate attention has also been given to the logistics of getting the troops into their appropriate positions, and ensuring adequate food and ammunition supplies. Furthermore, success will not be forthcoming unless the general receives continuous information that tells him whether the troops are deployed as intended, and whether the enemy is behaving as expected.

Figure 4.1 suggests that there should be a step-by-step approach to the leadership of change, and this is indicated by the solid lines connecting the boxes on the diagram (and also by the acronym itself). The dotted lines indicate two things. First, each step continues in parallel with each new step: this is particularly true of the charismatic and behavioural aspects, which should carry on beyond the change itself. The vision, for example, does not cease to be important because the change has been made effective. Or to continue the army example, the officers do not stop inspiring the troops because the ammunition has arrived. What is vital is that the change process begins with envisioning, and proceeds in a clockwise direction. Leapfrogging the steps can cause major problems, as the omission of any step can frustrate the whole change.

The second implication of the dotted lines is that each step, may force a reconsideration of the previous stages. An obvious example is that the control process under the heading 'Ensuring' might reveal issues that affect the detailed plans, or even force a reconsideration of the vision itself.

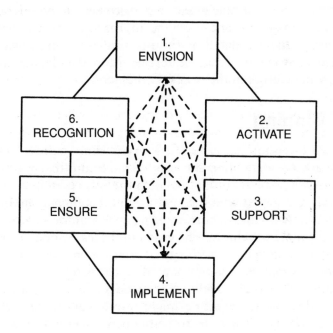

Figure 4.1 *EASIER approach to the leadership of fundamental change*

The implicit assumption is that change under this model is led by one person, and this may often be the case. However, the steps of the model are just as valid for change led by a team. It also makes sense for managers who are leading change and who are good at only some of the steps to extend their capabilities by deliberately using other people to supply the missing skills.

In a complex major change, the model may be applied at different levels in, or areas of, the organization. Size and complexity will dictate that responsibility for implementing the change has to be delegated. In this situation, a key task is to ensure that the whole process is both co-ordinated and follows the overall vision for the change.

The elements of the model are discussed in broad terms below, as it is important to see the approach as a whole before looking in greater detail at the practical ways in which the elements of the model may be applied. More detailed consideration will be given in the next two chapters.

envisioning

The word 'vision' has been used several times before. In this context it means a coherent view of the future that forms an over-arching objective for the organization. In this sense it might be compared with the famous 'I have a dream' speech of Martin Luther King, the dream being a view of the society that he was aiming to achieve. The vision of the leader of an organization may cover such things as size, scope of activities, economic strengths, relationships with customers and internal culture. It should also embrace the values of the organization, and to this extent the vision might inspire cultural as well as strategic change. It may be to be the best in certain fields: the best innovator, the most effective producer or the best employer. Because we are dealing with the management of change, in this context we are talking about a vision of a future that differs from the present.

The vision is usually inspired by a realization that a change is necessary. It may be inspired by the external forces that were discussed in the first chapter, or it may represent the leader's belief that the organization would do better if it operated in a different way. Later we will look at some of the characteristics of a good vision.

Defining the vision clearly is an important element in the leadership of change. The leader that cannot articulate the vision in a way that has meaning to others will face great difficulty in ensuring that everyone pulls in the same direction. It is easy to see how a poorly defined vision from the top could lead to numerous variations in interpretation as it was interpreted at different levels in the organization, which in turn could distort the implementation of the change.

As described here, vision gives the feeling of a total view of what the organization is trying to become at some point in the future. This is an appropriate starting place for the formulation of corporate strategies, but not all fundamental change requires such a complete view of the desired future state.

The downsizing of an operation may be accompanied by a vision that is concerned more with a future cost position and internal culture than a view of products and markets. The manager of a business unit may face what for the unit is a fundamental change, and for which a vision should be formulated, but this may be a long way from the total vision for the whole organization.

One could argue that the more coherence there is between the vision for the whole organization and that of a unit, the better will be the chance of a successful change. However, practical considerations make it clear that any manager facing a fundamental change situation can use the vision step of this approach in relation to the particular unit. 'Unit', for these purposes, may be a division, business, profit centre or cost centre.

An inappropriate vision can frustrate the change. The warning can be seen by looking at other words that have an association with those used to describe the concept. A dream is sometimes a nightmare, and a vision may be no more than a fantasy. Having a vision for the organization is good; claiming to see visions is somewhat suspect, and goes along with hearing voices! A key role of the person leading the change is to think through the vision to ensure that it is both desirable and sound.

activating

One of the tasks of any leader is to activate the followers. In the context of this model, activation is the task of ensuring that others in the organization understand, support and eventually share the vision. The vision cannot be understood unless it is communicated, and it cannot be communicated unless it is defined in a coherent way. Initially, the task is to develop a shared vision among the key players in the task of implementation but, depending on the change strategy (see Chapter 1), the activating task could stretch as deep into the organization as possible.

Commitment to the vision is a prerequisite for success, particularly among the people who have a key role in turning the vision into reality. Even in situations where a dictatorial approach to change is appropriate, the leader will not be able to undertake every task, and success is more likely if the key lieutenants are committed to the cause. But as we have seen, dictatorial approaches are only appropriate in certain circumstances, and most organizations will want to ensure that motivation is at a high level both before and after the change has been implemented. Even when the changes cause people to lose their jobs, this is more acceptable to them and to their surviving colleagues when they support the underlying vision that has led to this situation.

Figure 2.1 polarized the key people into those hostile to the change, who might well try to sabotage the process, and those who did not agree but supported it out of loyalty. It is, of course, possible for there to be a shared commitment to a vision and disagreement over the means chosen to achieve it, but for present purposes we could modify Figure 2.1 to examine the level of acceptance of the vision.

There is no doubt that progress towards the vision may be more difficult if it is opposed; at worst, the actions to implement it may be frustrated and the vision never achieved. More likely, there will be delays in implementation, and the path to success may be littered with management casualties. Leaders may be forced to be more coercive or dictatorial than they would have preferred, which may enable the change to be achieved but at the cost of poor morale in the organization during and after the change. The manager who implements actions out of loyalty, fear or some other motivation may be dangerous in a different sense. If the vision is not accepted, actions may be implemented by rule rather than with intelligence, and the fine-tuning of actions, essential in most change situations, may never take place. Doing what one is told is not always the same as acting with intelligence. It may be impossible for such managers to build a shared commitment to the vision among the people in their area of responsibility.

supporting

Good leadership is not just about telling people what to do. It is much more about inspiring them to do more than they otherwise might achieve, and providing the necessary moral and practical support to enable this to happen.

To achieve this, leaders must have a strong empathy with the people they are trying to inspire, and the imagination to see things from their point of view. There needs to be an understanding of both their present capabilities and their potential. While giving support to help a subordinate reach a tough new goal, a leader has to be able to recognize the problems the person faces, without ever implying that there is the slightest doubt that the person will succeed. Many of the principles of situational leadership are appropriate here, with the response to individuals being adjusted to their own level of capability and degree of motivation.

The concept of the inspiring and supportive leader who takes the followers to great achievements is well established in our culture, in history, myth and fiction. To some degree it may be a matter of pure charisma, with neither the leader nor the follower quite understanding why these feelings occur. My argument is that conscious attention to giving support and encouragement is part of the armoury of the leader of a change, and should not be a matter of chance.

There is a danger when the person leading the change lacks integrity or is insincere. Pretending to give encouragement, when it is clear that the leader does not really care and is merely performing a ritual, is likely to be counter productive. Support works when it is built on a base of respect, trust and integrity; it fails when these essentials are lacking.

Before discussing the three management headings of the approach, I should like to illustrate the complexity of implementing fundamental change, in particular gaining cultural change to support a new vision, with an example.

example: British Telecom

British Telecom has been undergoing a continuous process of change that began in 1990 and has been widely reported at various stages of the process. The vision of British Telecom is to become the most successful world-wide telecommunications group. The trigger for changes was a mix of external pressures and internal constraints, which, by 1990, had reached a point where the chief executive felt that action had to be taken. External pressures included the pace of technological change, with a 30 per cent annual fall in the costs of telecommunications as new technologies became available. The complexity of the telecommunications industry had increased to the point where it was difficult to see the joins with other industries, such as computers. The degree of turbulence in the environment had increased dramatically. Internally there was a mismatch of the organization and its old public utility culture compared to the vision and the realities of the external world. Managers' perceptions were not always appropriate, and the culture was introspective and controlling rather than outward looking and proactive.

The desired strategic change included a need to alter the culture of the organization. Before the change strategy was implemented the culture was prescriptive, with individuals being expected to conform to requirements. The desired change was to a culture that enabled individuals to excel, with the company providing the support that made this possible. At the same time there was a need to reduce the number of jobs, partly to reduce costs, and partly to enable the organization to be more customer responsive. The new structure would remove nine layers of management.

In early 1990 the chairman addressed the top 300 managers. They were told that the organization would change over the next 12 months, and that all 36,000 managers would take on new jobs. They were informed that there would be fewer jobs, and that the new organization would be in place by 1 April 1991. A team was set up to implement the changes.

After four months, organizational design had become an industry in its own right. Many of those involved in this new 'industry' were demonstrating the behaviours that the new design was intended to remove, such as the withholding of information, arbitrary decision making and a growth in bureaucracy. This led to a measure of cynicism within the organization. A survey was made that showed that actions were at odds with the vision, help was needed if managers were to behave differently, the whole process had made people more inward looking and that individuals were seeking sustained and continuous leadership from the board.

One result of this survey was the introduction of a two-and-a-half-day leadership programme. Six hundred managers had been through the programme by 1 April 1991, and the chairman had been heavily involved. The rest of the managers had seen a video presentation, with a board member present to answer questions.

By early 1992 there was a widespread recognition that the business was more turbulent, that most senior managers had been operating operationally rather than strategically, and a level of awareness had been developed among many people to enable them to participate in translating the group strategy to action.

Much of this change process was highly visible, because of the high profile of the company. The need for communication and effort to build shared values is clear from what happened, as is the need to train people to enable them to play the right part in the changed situation. Also clear is the length of time needed to change values in a long-established organization.

The example illustrates the difficulty a chief executive faces in converting his own vision to something that is shared throughout the group. In British Telecom's case, the problem was probably harder because the organization has always been profitable, and the need to change to fit the world of the future is not necessarily seen by all those in the organization.

Although the size of British Telecom makes the problem of leading change somewhat harder, what it experienced was not a unique situation, and the implications are of value to organizations of all sizes.

This example is modified from my book *Strategic Management: From Theory to Implementation* (see further reading) and includes extensive extracts from that work.

Sun Tzu, some 2,500 years ago in China, wrote a treatise on war that offers much good advice on strategy and leadership to the manager of today. Indeed, it has been reported as being essential reading in most Japanese boardrooms. One of his five points for victory is: 'He whose ranks are united in purpose will be victorious.' This can be used as a summary of what the first three letters of the EASIER approach deal with: defining a purpose and uniting people to achieve.

Sun Tzu also takes us to the second part of the acronym, management:

> In the tumult and uproar, the battle seems chaotic, but there must be no disorder in one's own troops. The battlefield may seem in confusion and chaos, but one's array must be in good order. That will be proof against defeat. Apparent confusion is a product of good order: apparent cowardice, of courage; apparent weakness of strength. Order or disorder depends on organization and direction; courage or cowardice on circumstances; strength or weakness on tactical dispositions.
>
> Used with permission of Sterling Publishing Co. Inc., 387 Park Ave. S., New York, NY 10016 from *Sun Tzu's Art of War*, © 1987 by General Tao Hanzhang.

How do we provide order and direction, and set the tactical dispositions to enable the change to be effected? The answer lies in the next three components of the model.

implementing

The implementing step is about the detailed plans and schedules that have to be completed to turn any vision into reality. The instruments themselves will vary, depending on the nature of the change and the length of time available to achieve it, but the basic reason is constant. It is to:

- Ensure that all the consequences of the change are understood, insofar as they can be foreseen.
- Identify all the actions that have to be taken to bring about the change. Here the discussion and methods of the previous chapter are relevant, to help ensure that nothing is overlooked.
- Allocate responsibility for the various actions that have to be taken.
- Establish the priorities of the various actions, in particular those that will hold up the whole process if not done to time.

■ Provide the budgets needed to ensure implementation of the plans.

■ Set up the teams and structures needed to implement plans.

■ Allocate the right human resources to the tasks (if necessary recruiting additional people or using consultants).

■ Setting goals for the change programme.

■ Determining any policies that are needed to make the implementation process work.

There is nothing unique or special about any of these individual requirements, or about the instruments, such as plans, budgets, critical path analysis, Gantt charts or other tools, that have to be developed to ensure that nothing is overlooked and everything is co-ordinated. These are all the regular instruments of management.

The difference is that the change may be so fundamental that all previous plans and schedules are worthless, and history may offer little guidance as to what needs to be done in the new situation. If the organization has never previously delayered, changed culture, outsourced many of its internal departments, drastically altered its structure, attempted a process of total quality management (TQM), transferred production from many plants to a single factory, developed strategic relationships with suppliers or customers, or... (the list is endless), then planning all the large and small intricate patterns of actions needed to ensure success may be much more difficult than past experience with planning might suggest.

---

example: some lessons from research

1. The KPMG acquisition survey mentioned in the previous chapter found that when making acquisitions, often one of the most difficult change areas to manage, many companies had 'inadequate measures for budgeting for

restructuring costs and measuring progress.' The assumption is often made, without justification, that a change can be achieved without expense, and lack of provision may make it impossible for a change to take place in an effective manner.

2. Lest you think that organizations automatically use the concepts, discussed in this and the previous chapter, to integrate all the elements of the change, let me mention some research by Professor Kaplan in 1995. He found that many organizations 'have a fundamental disconnect between the development and formulation of their strategy and the implementation of that strategy into useful action.' Four major barriers to effective implementation were identified.

■ Vision that could not be actioned because it was not translated into operational terms.

■ Strategy is not linked to departmental and individual goals (incentives are tied to financial performance instead of to long range strategy: only 22% of executive management and 6% of middle management have objectives that are tied to the strategy).

■ Resource allocation is based on short-term budgets and not the strategy (only just over a third of organizations have a direct link between the strategy and the budgeting process).

■ Control is directed at short-term performance and rarely evaluates progress on long-term objectives.

Professor Kaplan was researching implementation issues of the corporate strategies, each of which may encompass numerous other organizational change situations, but the point I want to stress comes through.

ensuring

Plans, structures for implementation, and policies may be formulated. On paper the organization may have covered everything. But this is not enough, and the ensuring part of the model is about establishing monitoring and controlling processes to ensure that:

■ All actions are taken on time, unless there is a conscious decision to change the actions.
■ Where actions are changed, there is good reason for the change and re-planning for the new circumstances.
■ The results of actions are as expected, or if not, that corrective action is taken (see the British Telecom example on pages 76–78, where results were different and new actions had to be taken).
■ The plans are still appropriate if the situation has changed.

All organizations have monitoring and controlling processes, but those that currently exist may be inadequate to monitor the change programme. One of the actions in the implementing phase might, therefore, have been to establish supplementary controls so that timely information is made available on a regular basis. When considering controls, attention should be given to qualitative issues as well as the quantitative. It may, for example, be as important to survey periodically the morale in the organization as to measure whether a new strategy has brought the expected reduction in unit costs.

Monitoring and control sound like cold, clinical processes. In fact, they can also be used as a reason for the various teams concerned in the change to meet on a frequent and regular basis, and as a means of reinforcing the commitment to the vision.

recognizing

The final step in the change leadership model is giving recognition to those involved in the process. Recognition may be positive or negative, and should be used to reinforce the change and to ensure that obstacles to progress are removed.

Although recognition may include financial reward, this may be the smallest part of what is needed. Public recognition (among peers and senior managers) of the part played by a particular manager may show that what has been done is appreciated. Promotion of someone who has played a major role may be a consequence of the performance in helping to implement the change. That small word 'thanks' may have great motivational value when expressed sincerely by a leader who is respected by the person. Failure to recognize an important contribution by someone may cause resentment, or a belief that the person is not valued.

It may be necessary to recognize certain negative aspects, such as the transfer of a valuable person who opposes the changes to a role where it is not possible to damage the change process. In some cases it may include the dismissal of a particular person who is frustrating the change or causing the pace to slow. Many fundamental change situations bring this type of casualty. Although more attention to creating commitment to the vision might avoid some of these problems, it would be unrealistic to suggest that there will never be management casualties.

Russian dolls

Because it is easier to describe in this way, much of the discussion of this approach to leadership is from the viewpoint of the chief executive of the organization. In fact, the approach has a wider application than this and one way of visualizing it is to think of the key people in the change process as a series of nested Russian dolls. To take the analogy further, try to visualize all the dolls, except the one on the outside, as wrapped in a plastic skin.

The chief executive, the outside doll, has the ability to develop strategy, structure, process and culture in support of the vision. Indeed, the vision will be no more than an empty dream unless this happens. Figure 4.2 offers a minor adaptation to Figure 3.3 on page 55 by changing the box 'desired change' to 'strategies', and nesting the whole model within a six-sided figure that shows the steps that make up the EASIER approach. For the chief executive the overall organizational aspects of the model are subservient to the vision, and are the way in which some of the steps in the change leadership model are converted to results. There is not a one-for-one correlation between the headings in the two models; strategies to enable the vision to be attained are clearly part of the implementation step. The strategies themselves may be used to help refine the vision, and the strategic planning process itself may be used to gain commitment to the vision. Similar multiple relationships could be developed for the other boxes in the integrated organizational model.

This is a different position to a senior manager who reports to the chief executive. The change leadership model is just as valid for that person except that it has to be applied in the context of the total organization. In a sense this is the plastic skin that separates the dolls in the analogy. There may be many elements where this next doll in the hierarchy has wide strategic freedom as, for example, the head of a major strategic business unit, but that freedom has to be exercised in the context of the total organizational vision, strategies and other components of the organizational model. At the same time, the actions of this strategic business unit (SBU) chief executive form the skin in which the next Russian doll operates. We could carry the analogy down to the last position in the hierarchy, that tiny, last doll that is eventually discovered many layers inside the toy.

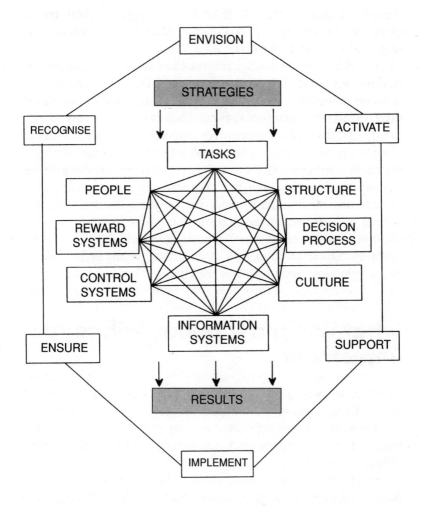

Figure 4.2 *The EASIER approach to change and the integrated organization*

There may be a need to lead fundamental change at any point in the hierarchy. Sometimes this may be playing a role to take the corporate vision into all the corners of the total organization. Thus every business stream in BP went through its own change process to align itself with the Project 1990 initiative mentioned in earlier chapters. But a fundamental change may also occur at one of the lower levels. An SBU head may need to change the SBU cost base for competitive reasons, and this change may not extend beyond the SBU; the information systems manager may take his or her department through a fundamental philosophical change (such as out-sourcing, developing a customer responsive approach to the internal customers, or some equally complex change that would affect the whole information systems (IS) activity). The model is equally valid for this manager, except that whatever is done has to fit within the context of the overall organization. If the value system of the whole organization puts great store on the way employees are treated, the IS manager would have to ensure that this value was applied in the handling of any redundancies that might occur as a result of the change.

what we know about failure to implement

Many concepts have been developed from the study of successful change, and the model presented in this chapter is a synthesis of the findings of many of the authors who have led the thinking in this area. Lessons can also be learnt from failure.

The findings used here came from a study by Larry Alexander (see 'Strategy implementation: the nature of the problem' in D E Hussey (editor), *International Review of Strategic Management*, 2(1), 1991).

The following 10 points deal specifically with why organizations fail to implement the strategies in their plans (which of course does not cover every aspect of change). The headings below, which are in the respondents' order of importance, come from the research, but the supporting narrative is my interpretation. The point at the top was noted by 76 per cent of the sample, while the tenth item was still found in 56 per cent. So we are not stretching the data to points noted by only a minority of organizations.

1. Implementation took longer than planned. This deals with the implementation part of the leadership model and the failure, discussed in Chapter 3, to think through all the things that had to be done. It may also relate to the lack of a quick response system for monitoring and controlling, so that corrective action to catch up was not taken in time. Something that takes longer may cause other adverse results, such as extra costs or a loss of customer confidence (an example is the Passport Office computerization discussed on pages 2–3).

2. Major problems surfaced that had not previously been identified. This again is a failure to think through all implications and consequences of the change, and takes us back to the example of the Child Support Agency on pages 5 and 24. It could also be that the vision was flawed, because not enough effort had been made to make it a reality. We should not delude ourselves into believing that the unexpected will never happen, but many organizations experience surprises from consequences that could have been foreseen.

3. There was inadequate co-ordination of implementation activities. This could be because too little effort had gone into defining the actions that had to be taken to implement; or because the vision was not shared by the key people, so that too many of the implementation actions were aiming in different directions, with different priorities. It could be that the decisions in the boardroom had not filtered down to the actions of those at the coalface.

4. Competing activities and crises diverted attention so that the decisions were not implemented. One can only assume that the strategies were not formulated with a clear vision.

5. Managers lacked the capabilities needed to implement. This indicates a failure of the support and implementation stages.

6. Training and instruction given to lower-level employees was inadequate. This could be because of lack of understanding of the implications of the change, disagreement with the strategy by the managers, or a reflection of the inadequacies of the managers themselves.

7. Uncontrollable external factors had a detrimental impact on implementation. Reality or perception? Some might argue that the problems experienced by the Child Support Agency were caused by a level of hostility to it that could not be foreseen. My belief is that most of the problems could have been anticipated and avoided, and that this is a case of flawed vision and inadequate implementation processes. Of course, the unexpected can occur, and leaders have to be responsive to events. Strategies may be inadequate to attain the vision, and may need to be changed. But it is always easier to blame our own deficiencies on an external cause.

8. Departmental managers gave inadequate leadership and direction. This could be due to sheer lack of ability, but more probably resulted from a failure in the activating stage. If the key managers do not share the vision, they may be incapable of helping to lead their part of the change process.

9. Key implementation tasks were not defined in sufficient detail. It is clear which part of the model is at fault here. It also relates to the Kaplan research discussed earlier in this chapter, which showed that

the strategies and the control drivers of short-term performance were not aligned in too many organizations.

10. Information systems were inadequate for monitoring implementation. Failure to give attention to this at the outset is akin to trying to drive a car that has no petrol gauge or speedometer. The journey might be frustrated by over-cautiousness, the car might run into a police speed trap, or it might run out of fuel.

This top-10 listing came from a survey of private sector companies. There were a few differences when the survey was repeated among public sector organizations. In addition, the resistance of employees to implementation because it conflicted with their personal goals was noted, and overall goals that were not well enough understood by employees were a further serious problem.

---

example: British Gas

Early in 1999 British Gas announced that it was to close its retail sales operations almost with immediate effect, as they were losing money. This true story illustrates the sort of difficulties that can result when those at the sharp end are either not fully informed of the change, are opposed to it, or are not trained so that they could implement it properly. You can call it a teething problem if you wish, making allowances for the sheer size of the organization, or you can interpret it as something that had not been properly worked out before the first steps of the change were made.

An elderly lady, who is in her 90s, living in sheltered accommodation, had her gas fire condemned during a routine gas service. This was at the time when the local gas showroom had recently closed. Her daughter helped her to obtain a replacement. The first step was to telephone British Gas. You need not be bored by the story of how many calls had to be made. It is enough to say that on the first call to the customer services number she was told that British Gas no longer sold appliances. Only the perseverance of the customer eventually led to someone who was able to explain the new system that was being used to sell gas appliances.

This would require a personal visit from a technical sales advisor, which was efficiently arranged over the telephone. On the morning of the visit the sales advisor phoned to say he did not want to come, but as the daughter had travelled 40 miles to be with her mother at the time of the visit he eventually agreed. When he arrived at the appointed time, he handed over a brochure but said that he could give no help as, although he was now responsible for selling and advising about these appliances, all he knew was central heating. He then spent more than 30 minutes on a monologue about the chaos in the system and the stupidity of his employers in expecting people to do jobs they knew nothing about.

My interpretation of this story is that it illustrates points 3, 6 and 9 above, and possibly points 1 and 8 too. It is very likely that the closure of shops and the resultant employee redundancies may have been handled well. But the positive aspect of the change, the continued sale of gas appliances by another method, seemed not to have had the same attention. The people who interfaced with customers seemed to be out of step with the boardroom.

Am I being unkind when I suggest that use of the approaches discussed so far would have removed many of the problems identified in the research and reinforced by the example? The next two chapters will dwell more on the 'how' of applying the EASIER approach.

envisioning, activating and supporting in practice

This chapter provides some checklists of points to consider when applying the Envisioning, Activating and Supporting elements of the EASIER model which, as we have seen, are the leadership and behavioural aspects for achieving fundamental change. The rationale of each of the elements has been discussed in the previous chapter, and we are now left with the practical issues of what should be done to help make the model work.

The assumption of this chapter and the next is that the reader is leading the change, because the approach is appropriate at any level of the organization that is undergoing fundamental change. Those readers not currently managing a change situation might like to compare what is said here with their experience of change in their own organizations.

There are four prerequisites for using the approach:

1. Do you know your own strengths and weaknesses? This is important because it may mean that you need to ensure that you have help at certain stages of the change process, using the abilities of others to reinforce areas where you know you are weak. It may also mean that you have rapidly to acquire some additional skills in order to be successful. It may mean that you have to apply some self-discipline to curb aspects of your normal behaviour that might frustrate the process. (For example, at the activating stage you may need to encourage subordinates to challenge your vision. If your normal style is to discourage such challenges you may have to take a deep breath and modify your own behaviour.)

2. Have you determined the degree of resistance and the urgency of the change, so that you can select the best approach? Refer back to Chapter 1 if you need more information about this.

3. Do you have good internal and external information that is relevant to the change and will enable you to formulate a sound vision? Creative thinking and insight are important, but by themselves are rarely enough to ensure that a vision is relevant.

4. Do you fully understand the trigger for the change? Obviously, change is unlikely unless someone has seen a need for it, and this need has to be correctly seen and thoroughly understood. If the trigger is misinterpreted, the proposed changes may take the organization in the wrong direction.

envisioning

A well-stated vision statement provides a platform for understanding the organization, a sort of map reference for what it is about. It should also give emotional appeal, so that others want to share the future that the vision offers. Both these roles of vision should be born in mind when thinking about the components of a good vision.

points to consider in formulating a vision

1. Is the vision credible? To be credible, it must be grounded in the reality of the market and the general business situation the organization faces, and the resources that the organization can command. If the vision is unrealistic the change may fail because it cannot be achieved. If others in the organization cannot see it as relevant, their lack of acceptance may cause the change to fail. If you think about the BP example again, it is clear that the way the internal working parties were set up, and the results discussed, meant that the vision was based on a sound perception of the market. It was widely seen as a relevant way of dealing with the situation.

2. Is it challenging? To be too challenging may be to lose credibility; not to be challenging enough may be to lose the emotional appeal that the vision should have. Words, such as 'inspiring', 'stretching' and 'exhilarating', have all been used by various authorities to describe this aspect of the vision. Something that can excite the organization is more likely to succeed than a boring statement that looks as if it will not lead to anything that will take the organization to a better place.

3. Does it have internal integrity? By this I mean do the various elements of the vision fit together without contradicting each other? In a complex situation this may be far more difficult to achieve than it may appear at first sight.

4. Is it clear? A vision that lacks clarity may be difficult to communicate to others, and may also mean that the wrong strategies will be formulated to achieve it. The vision should be complete enough to ensure that it is sound, and should leave people in no doubt of what the organization will be like if it achieves the vision. Later it may be possible to encapsulate the vision into a slogan. Komatsu developed a well-thought-out vision for out-performing the US giant Caterpillar, and laid the ground well in its supporting strategies. Once this was done it was possible to get the whole organization aligned behind one slogan, 'Encircle Caterpillar'. The slogan would have been meaningless had it not been based on a sound vision.

5. How does the vision relate the past, present and future? A fundamental change usually implies some discontinuity with the past trends, and often it is the discontinuity that justifies all the actions that have to be taken to achieve the new vision. At the same time, denying the past may create a situation where longer-serving employees feel resentful. If it is possible to build a bridge from where the company is now to where it needs to be, praising past successes while emphasizing the need for change, the vision may be much more acceptable to the organization. Beware of the trap of blaming the present situation on the poor decisions of your predecessors: this common management misbehaviour can be totally counter-productive.

6. Do you believe in the vision? If you do not believe in the vision to the point where achieving it is the most important task you face, you will have difficulty in both holding on to it yourself and convincing others. Where you have complete freedom you should have few problems here. However, when the vision you formulate for your area is in the context of a broader organizational vision that you do not share, you may

have to think very hard about whether you should be pressing ahead with changes until you are convinced that the overall direction is right.

barriers to overcome

Although the vision may look sound, there can be barriers that prevent it from being an effective driver for change:

1. Does the vision meet most of the above criteria? If not you may need to face up to the fact that you need help from others to formulate it. There is no reason why the development of the vision has to be a one-person activity, and sometimes a small team will achieve better results. In many situations allowing others to participate fully in the whole change process can be a powerful force for achieving success. However, remember that it is not always possible to gain unanimous agreement to a vision, as people may have different views of the situation. So although all comments should be taken seriously, and may modify your own initial ideas, if you are managing the situation you will have to make the final decision about what is required
2. Do day-to-day actions reinforce the vision? If short-term issues are more important than the longer-term aspects of the vision, it may be that, however wonderful the vision looks, it is not appropriate for the organization at this time.
3. Does every aspect of your own behaviour reinforce the vision? In most organizations there is a degree of cynicism, and any implication that you are not committed to the vision may be used as a reason for not accepting it. 'Moral for top management: Do not announce the "new culture" until and unless you are the best

example' (Larry Farrell, *Searching for the Spirit of Enterprise*, Dutton, New York, 1991).

4. Have the implications of the vision been thought through? Do you really understand where the vision will lead you, and what it may mean in the types of change that are necessary within the organization? The example of the Child Support Agency showed that although the vision of the new initiative appeared sound, the implications of many aspects of the change were not considered.

5. Can the vision be converted to strategies and actions? This is part of the implementation stage, but at the time of forming the vision you must have a clear idea of the type of actions that will be needed.

---

example: Marks and Spencer plc

Marks and Spencer has built an almost unique position in the eyes of its customers and the public at large, with an image of fairness to customers and as a good employer. As long ago as 1974, Sir Marcus Sieff, the then chairman, said in his annual report:

> We believe that if we guard the standards of our goods, improve our systems and look after our staff and our customers, we shall continue to grow and to make profits.

We need profits after paying taxes:

1. To improve the pay and working conditions of our staff and to take care of them during retirement. The high morale and productivity of our staff owes much to these factors; most of them take pride in working for a successful business which is quality oriented

2. To have funds for investment in the development of the business, which is clearly desired by our many customers;

3. To pay a proper dividend to our 240,000 shareholders, which include many small savers, individual pensioners and pension funds.

Many companies make similar statements in their annual reports. The difference is that Marks and Spencer lived these statements, had done so for many years before 1974, and continued to do so until at least 1998, when the profit growth machine faltered.

The vision described by Sir Marcus was recognizable by customers and staff, and the many changes the organization went through followed this guiding light. The move into financial services can only be described as a fundamental change, and was made possible partly because of the reputation of the firm. The acquisition of a US retailer was a fundamental change. Expansion of the store network was largely incremental.

From late 1998, and particularly during 1999, the firm began undergoing many new changes. The problem the firm faced was a reduction of revenue and profitability, rather than actual losses, following a worrying trend as shoppers seemed to be deserting the stores. Turnaround situations usually present a great challenge to management. On the one hand change may become more acceptable as the whole organization sees the obvious need. However, there is usually a problem in that the whole pattern of change can rarely be seen at the outset, and instead of moving from a current vision to a clearly stated future vision, the changes are likely to be jerky, as sequential decisions are made to bring immediate improvements.

Where the overall vision is hard to see, it becomes difficult to provide a clear vision for each specific change as it is formulated. It makes it more likely that change actions will not be as well co-ordinated as they should be. The overall task facing M & S appeared to have three elements: cutting out some unprofitable overseas operations; reducing costs so that they were more closely aligned to the level of turnover; getting customers back into the stores in the UK. The hardest of these, which is also the task of greatest long-term importance, is the last.

Not surprisingly many change actions have resulted from Marks and Spencer's new situation. There have been waves of redundancies as employment levels were reduced. Although this is upsetting in any organization, it is a reasonable assumption that the people leaving have been well treated. The public is used to reading newspaper reports of such events, and the need to reduce does not impair the company's image. The cancellation of offers of appointment to the 55 students who had been offered places only a few months earlier was a different matter. It became a human-interest story that was widely reported in the press, with most articles being hostile. As outsiders we can see that there must be good reasons for not recruiting graduates in a year of redundancies, but it is hard to see why the decision was not taken before the recruitment activity took place. This is the sort of issue that could drip poison into the veins of M & S's greatest asset: the trust that customers have in the firm. It raises the question of whether the changes are following a new coherent vision.

Marks and Spencer have had long-term relationships with their suppliers. Of course all retailers buy in the goods they sell, but the relationship that M & S have had is much closer to the sort of strategic alliance recommended in the modern thinking about outsourcing. It was, therefore, a surprise when in October 1999 they terminated a relationship of many years' standing with a manufacturer that had supplied much of their clothing and which had the majority of its business with M & S. Some 4,000 employees of this supplier are likely to lose their jobs as a result. Shortly afterwards came the news of a number of other cancelled contracts with suppliers. Also in October came the announcement of the relocation of the head office from its long established site in Baker Street, London.

The questions that all this poses are: 'What is the vision of M & S today and what is its strategy?' 'If these are in any way lacking, will it be possible for the key managers at M & S to develop a motivating vision for each major change?' And 'If this cannot be done, would the image of M & S in the eyes of its former customers alter so much that it becomes even harder to entice them back into the stores?' The future success of M & S of course depends on the quality of the decisions taken about change, but the implementation of those decisions requires a new shared vision for those who work in the company.

activating

Even when a dictatorial approach to change is justified, it is rare that everything is done by one person. Most change situations require involvement from at least the key people, and often there is a need to 'sell' the vision of the change to the whole organization. In some situations, shareholders, customers, suppliers and bankers may need to be convinced that a workable vision, properly supported, really does exist. The activating phase is important in all change situations, the debate being the choice of who should share the vision and the methods used to achieve this. There can be few successful change situations where leaders have not convinced anyone else of their vision for the change and its outcomes.

There are questions of timing. Sometimes it is not practical to introduce the change into every area of the organization at the same time, so a phased approach may be possible. In a small organization or unit it may be possible for the leader to work individually and collectively with everyone. However, an organization does not have to get very large before the leader of the change has to delegate parts of the activating process to others. This means that the activating task should begin at the senior levels some time before the change is put into effect. For lower levels of the organization the gap in time between building commitment to the vision and disclosing the detail of the change should not be long, particularly if some people are to lose their jobs. It is just as unfair to create unnecessary stress and uncertainty when this can be avoided, as it is to inspire people with the vision of a new shared future only days before they are made redundant.

The activating task should be carefully planned, the decisions on timing and delegation of the task being contingent on the situation.

Some of the methods that may be used to communicate the vision and build support for it are listed below. There is room for choice, as not all situations will require the same response, and some of the methods shown here have already been illustrated in the BP and BT examples. A further example will appear after we have looked at these methods.

ways of activating the organization

1. Demonstrate your own belief in the vision and feeling of excitement about it all the time. Although the gestures, like holding internal conferences, may provide platforms for the set speeches, remember that judgements are formed not on what you say but on how you behave. Think for a moment about your views of the policies of the national political parties: the grand speeches are important, but the real view you form is based on something more than rhetoric. It is what the day-to-day actions mean. Now extend this to business organizations. What percentage of those company chairmen who have stated 'Our people are our greatest asset' are stating something that those inside the organization see as credible? The vision is reinforced not only by your day-to-day actions, but also by the opportunity you take to mention aspects of it in the numerous regular contacts that you have with peers and subordinates.

2. Extend personal contact as far as possible through the organization, to communicate your own sense of excitement and to explain the vision. Most successful major changes have involved a high degree of 'managing by walking about', ensuring that everyone understands the vision, or those aspects that relate to

their job, and building a sense of trust in management and of belonging. Do this even though you may be relying on others in the organization to share the activating task.

3. Workshops of key people are a valuable way of building commitment, and allowing them to participate in the process. If the vision is defined, a typical workshop might find opportunities for people to test the vision, help define its implications, and decide how to build commitment at lower levels. Such workshops may provide an element of education in the tools and methods needed, and should result in action plans. The word 'workshop' was used here instead of 'conference', because this approach is valid for organizations of all sizes and is not restricted to changes at corporate level. The best advice I can give for planning a workshop is to ensure that the participants have plenty of opportunity to work on the issues of the workshop; just listening to others talking about the new vision is unlikely to build commitment.

4. Ensure that there are opportunities for two-way communication. If all the communication is downwards, you may never know of serious concerns that people may have and that could have been dealt with had you known. There may also be information that would affect your thinking if it were shared with you. This means that you should be willing to admit errors when they exist (although if the vision has been properly thought through, these will be errors of implementation, not of direction). Never display anger if the vision appears to be criticized.

5. Supplement the personal messages with other media, such as the company newspaper, videos for internal use, personal letters to employees, e-mail, and voice-mail. Ensure that policy memos prepared by others

reflect the message you are trying to put over. Think through the whole communications strategy at the outset, for although it will not be possible to forecast every action, this will put you in position so that you can exploit every opportunity and maintain consistency in all communications.

6. Use the everyday meetings to emphasize the message. These opportunities may arise in various forms: strategy review meetings, monthly meetings to review progress against budget, routine management meetings, making time to speak at internal training meetings.

7. Consider how external public relations might aid internal communication and communication with the influencers outside, such as customers. This may be essential for large public organizations, if only to prevent negative publicity. British Gas, in 1994–95, must have wished that it had handled its PR a little differently, especially in co-ordinating the timing of its various decisions. Unrelated situations (top management pay increases coinciding with major redundancies, and administrative concerns) meant that external publicity made it more difficult for those inside the organization to manage the change process. Remember that major change in any large or well-known company or public sector organization is a matter of great interest to the public, and is difficult to keep secret. Although secrecy may be essential at certain points at the beginning of the change process, it is more sensible to manage media relations, ensuring that the messages you send out reinforce your intentions, and not to carry the secrecy claim beyond its reasonableness.

8. Seek out examples of success that reinforce the vision. These do not have to be the major strategic successes; for many people simpler, everyday events

may have more meaning. The head of SAS in his major turnaround of the 1980s gave many examples of how staff at the check-in counters had dealt with customer situations in a way that reinforced his vision of how the airline should operate.

9. Select your team members with care, and do not be afraid to take tough decisions to sideline or remove those who you fear might obstruct the change (but do this in a dignified and humane way). Be willing to empower the team, so that it can make a genuine contribution. The vision will never be shared if all issues have to be referred upwards. Trust has to be built between the proponent of the new vision and the key members of the team that will help to implement it.

10. Audit the nature and content of internal training to ensure that the key changes are reflected in the courses and that appropriate skills are provided for those who are affected by the changes.

barriers to overcome

1. Resistance to change needs to be identified and strategies developed to overcome it. This was discussed at some length in Chapter 2.

2. Lack of skill in the leader. At the beginning of this chapter I emphasized the need to take careful stock of your own strengths and weaknesses. One simple example is that of two-way communication skills: if these are absent, much of what has been discussed above would fail. Such skills can be learnt (to a degree), or the issue may be solved by having a partner in the change process, closely identified with you, who has the skills you lack.

3. Unwillingness to take tough decisions about individual people. If the vision is critical to the success of the

organization, it must not be frustrated by the behaviour of one or two key managers. Many managers may find it easier to deal with a massive downsizing decision than to face up to what to do with one hostile or inadequate manager who would otherwise frustrate the process. The reason is that the second action is very personal and may concern a respected colleague of long standing.

example: 'Premier Foods'

The name of the organization is disguised. It had many business units operating in many countries, and the change illustrated, although fundamental, was not accompanied by any redundancies. The initiator saw a need to change the priority placed on people if the overall vision of the organization were to be achieved, a key aspect being the introduction of a business driven approach to management development. The formulation of a vision for this change at head office level, without involving any of the diverse organizations involved, would have made the activating task very difficult. The initiator also obtained the backing of a senior, credible executive, who was to act as a top-level champion of the change. The next stage was the formation of a multinational task force to:

■ Make a realistic assessment of the current state of management development throughout the organization.
■ Define a vision for management development.
■ Develop a transition plan from the present to the desired vision.

The first step towards the activation stage was taken through a survey of what was currently going on in the diverse levels, functions and countries. The survey provided hard evidence that was used to demonstrate the need and validity for the change, and gave an opportunity to alert the managements of the various businesses that there was an issue.

A vision statement was developed of the desired future purposes of management development, and supported by an identification of the critical success factors, the new management competencies that would be needed, and the principles of management development. The task force eventually achieved unanimous agreement over these documents.

In reality the activating stage was already in progress, through the members of the task force and the work on the audit. However, something more was needed, and the main method chosen was what was termed the GOLD programme. This was a four-day programme, which cascaded through the organization, beginning with the whole executive team and then working through the management hierarchy. Members of the executive team, including the president, thereafter presented the visions and management development principles in the cascade sessions of the programme.

The aim of GOLD was to share awareness of the problems, to ensure that the vision was communicated widely, to build commitment to that vision, to achieve consistent application of the required skills and behaviours across the organization, and to convert the vision into numerous personal action plans.

In essence, GOLD was a process 'to achieve change in management development through partnership between line management, human resources and the individual'. In this process, management development was the means to achieve business performance and not an end in itself.

An additional method to activate the vision was the use of a small core from the task force to help address organizational inhibitors or potential blockages to the change. Part of their role was to pass to the organization information on successes.

Obviously these were only the main methods used. What was critical about them was that they built a genuine commitment to the new vision, because managers became convinced that it was soundly based and necessary. The final important matter is that it worked.

support

This is the behavioural underpinning to the whole process. In the Premier example support was given in a number of ways, one of which was by ensuring through the GOLD programme that all managers had the specific skills needed to make the new process work.

ways of giving support to people

1. Express confidence in subordinates and peers involved in the change. Ensure through the way you deal with people that they see that you have no doubt about their ability to deliver what is asked of them. At the same time ensure that you have been realistic when assigning tasks, and have done this with a full knowledge of their strengths, weaknesses and demands on their time.

2. Provide coaching to help them overcome difficulties. This is a mix of help and advice coupled with encouragement. Just as with a sports coach, the aim is to help subordinates to overcome new challenges.

3. Ensure that key people are properly empowered to play their part in the change process. This means giving clarity as to their role, authority and responsibility. It also means showing through your public actions that they are handling particular aspects, and that you are not involved on a day-to-day basis. It means avoiding negative criticism of subordinates because they did not handle the task in the way that you would have done it, although you should still hold them accountable for results.

4. Be empathetic to people's situations during the change process, but do not deviate from the main thrust of the change.

5. Use praise and thanks as a positive way to enhance motivation.

barriers to overcome

1. Lack of time. Major changes are demanding on time, both for the leader and the key members of the team. This is because the numerous new tasks are usually in addition the normal workload. Those extra things needed for support activity take yet more time, and it is both easy and erroneous to see them as less important than other tasks

2. Lack of consistency. Your behaviour to people on aspects of the change should not be different from your behaviour on day-to-day management. If your style to date has not included the type of actions suggested here, the worst thing you could do would be to continue normal behaviour on the day-to-day things, while being highly supportive of anything to do with the change. Behaviour has to be consistent, or you risk being seen in a cynical light.

applying the management elements of the EASIER approach

This chapter covers what can be termed the management aspects of the fundamental change process. All the tools and methods described here are in general use. Few of them can be considered relevant only in change situations. The important thing is to select the approaches that best fit the situation, and to ensure that the routines inside the organization are modified to take account of the change that is being implemented. Each of the three stages discussed in this chapter must be given careful thought during the change process, and no assumptions made about the suitability of existing procedures. It is important to know that the right management approaches are in place, not to assume that they are.

implementation

This is the detailed planning stage, when the broad vision is converted to strategies and detailed plans; goals (in the sense of milestones) are defined and responsibilities assigned. Not all the methods described here are right for every situation, and the person leading the change has to select what is needed for the particular change situation. Remember that this phase must contain not only the actions needed to achieve the vision but also those (such as overcoming resistance) that relate to the process of change. So we are planning not only what we must do, but also how we must do it.

1. strategic plans

The role strategic plans play will vary with the type of fundamental change. British Telecommunications' vision of moving from being a domestic telephone company to a major player in global communications could not have even begun to be implemented without some very careful strategic planning. A part of such a strategic change might well be a decision to have a leaner and more agile organization, and although this requires its own vision most of the related changes would require detailed operational action plans rather than a longer-term strategic plan. So to some degree the need for a strategic plan depends on where you are, the breadth of the vision and the length of time needed to attain the vision.

factors to consider when making strategic plans

1. The strategic plan should describe the means for attaining the corporate vision, dealing with the positioning of the organization and setting out strategic actions that must be taken.
2. The process of narrowing down the vision to specific objectives and developing strategies to achieve them can be used to gain commitment.

3. The plan is a management tool, and should give equal weight to analysis and the behavioural issues. Strategic decision making involves determining the options available, defining the probable consequences of each and making a choice. It is one way in which the consequences of the change can be thoroughly examined.

4. A good plan will also look at contingencies: what the effect might be if things did not turn out as forecast, and what should be done about it. You may recall that one criticism by the National Audit Office of the Passport Agency was a failure to provide a contingency plan, so when things started to go wrong, they continued to go wrong. The plan might be used by people who are not familiar with its background. The document should therefore be clear so that any authorized reader can understand the strategy.

5. Gaps in the strategy should be explicitly stated, and the necessary additional investigation should be one of the tasks arising from the plan.

common pitfalls to avoid in strategic plans

1. Plans too vague to enable implementation.

2. Plans examine only part of the issue and ignore other parts. For example, the cost and customer implications might have been considered, but not integrated with the necessary human resource issues.

3. Ambition outstrips ability: the plans cannot be implemented because the organization does not have the capability or resources.

4. Strategic plans underestimate the time needed to implement major change.

2. short-term plans and budgets

A strategic plan sets the framework, but more work is usually needed to break the actions down, to ensure that responsibility is properly delegated, and that authority is given for capital and revenue expenditures.

factors to consider when making short-term plans and budgets

1. The short-term plan should include descriptions of the actions being taken, and provide a financial description. It should cover qualitative issues as well as quantitative.
2. Make clear what actions are to be taken and who is to take them. If this is not done, people may either ignore key actions, assume that someone else is dealing with them, or find that two or more people have each started to do the same action, without co-ordination.
3. Set time limits and short-term goals to enable monitoring systems to be set up.
4. All organizations have some form of budgetary process, and this may sometimes be adequate for managing a fundamental change. However, it is more likely that a separate plan and budget will be required for a fundamental change, and that this should be the basis of managing the change as a project. In this case, the interface between the normal budgetary process and the project should be carefully thought out.
5. A project budget is likely to cross responsibility centres, and for this reason should give better management of a change that affects many areas of the organization than reliance on the more usual budget, which is focused on reaching total costs and revenues, but focus on individual responsibility centres.

common pitfalls to avoid in short-term plans and budgets

1. Treating financial issues as more important than

underlying actions and being satisfied when the numbers are achieved, even if the actions taken are the wrong ones.
2. Believing that budgets are only for accountants, when they should be tools for managers.
3. Failure to integrate short-term plans with strategy.
4. Failure to relate short-term plans to each other, for example, performance management systems and the annual plan.
5. Lack of guidance to all managers of responsibility centres so that they are unaware of the part they should be playing in the change, and cannot take this into account in their own plans and budgets.

3. project management

It may have already become clear that the types of plan discussed so far may be too broad to ensure that really complex change projects are properly managed. This is because none of the approaches discussed so far can accommodate the thousands of large and small actions needed to implement complex change; few cross departmental boundaries, though many projects involve a number of departments, and holding to the change priorities is difficult when the actions are mixed up with all the other tasks each manager has to fulfil. The steps listed above are essential, and sometimes may prove adequate, but in many situations something extra will be needed: project management.

factors to consider in project management
1. Responsibility for a project's success must be clearly delegated. This may be to an individual, or in certain situations to a self-directed team, but it must be clear that the project has to be managed. In really complex fundamental change there may be several simultaneous projects, each established with clear lines of

responsibility and authority. These may be indepen-
dent, or interdependent and nestling within a master
project. It may be that only a part of the overall change
requires a high level of project management skills
(such as the building of a new factory), while other
aspects (like a change in how customers are treated)
can be implemented through much simpler methods,
like action plans.

2. Decide how to organize the project team. A choice
must be made between a line-project organization,
with a permanent team brought together to manage
the project, and a matrix organization that uses
existing skills and resources from the organization
without full-time membership of the project team. The
former method may be best when the project is highly
focused, will require large resources of people over a
long time, or is of a confidential nature that has to
restrict knowledge of the project to the smallest
possible number of people. The matrix method makes
best use of scarce expertise, ensures maximum involvement of the organizational units that have to play a
part in the change, and is particularly appropriate
when expertise is needed for short periods and on a
part-time basis.

3. Either solution requires that the project is carefully
managed so that it identifies every action to be
performed, calculates the time and costs involved, and
schedules actions so as to achieve the shortest time to
completion (by, for example, running actions in
parallel whenever possible, ensuring actions that will
create delays are finished on time, and checking that
priorities are kept). Project management works to
defined goals of both time and results, and can subdi-
vide elements of the project into smaller projects, each
with a project manager.

4. Project management is also about information and

control, aspects that are discussed in the ensuring stage of the EASIER model.

5. Appropriate project management techniques should be used, although these may have application outside project management. It is convenient to consider two of them at this point.

technique 1: Gantt charts

The Gantt chart is a simple way of showing a number of tasks and the length of time needed to complete them. It can be used in strategic and short-term plans, as well as in project management, but is likely to deal with broadly defined actions. For example, in the annual plan all the human resource management actions in downsizing may be reduced to one or two broad headings, whereas detailed management of the project would identify numerous actions, each with its own time scale, some of which have to be finished before others can be started. It is not sensible to advise individuals that they are to be made redundant until (1) a fair selection has been made, and (2) the terms of redundancy have been decided. To decide the post-change staffing level requires a consideration of how the work will be organized. Depending on the nature of the organization, it may be necessary to consult with the trades unions before final decisions are reached.

By careful grouping on the chart it is possible to relate actions to each other. However, when the project is highly complex and time needs to be scheduled very accurately, the usefulness of the technique is reduced. It may still be appropriate for managing the actions within each area of the organization, but something more is needed to bring all the areas together into one plan.

technique 2: network analysis

There are many variants of network analysis, and the illustration here is to give the flavour of the approach rather than the full details. Networks tackle the problem where lots of actions

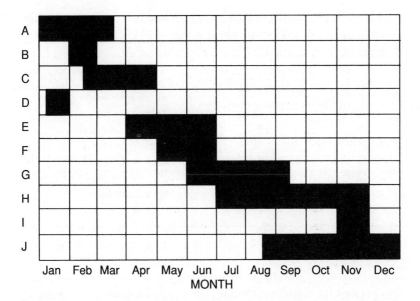

Figure 6.1 *Example of a Gantt chart showing action start and finish dates*

have to be undertaken and some have to be completed before others can be started. Having all this information and putting it into a diagram enables the work to be organized differently to eliminate bottlenecks, and prevents assumptions being made that rely on the same person being in two different countries at the same time. It also enables a critical path to be established that shows the order in which tasks have to be performed for the project to be completed in the quickest possible time.

The fact that a task will take six months is not critical if it can be started any time and the results are not needed until the last stage of the project. A much shorter task taking only a few days may be absolutely critical, in that many subsequent tasks are dependent on its performance. If completion of this task is delayed, the whole project will be late. The use of network analysis can be seen from looking at a simple situation and then projecting the principles to the more complex realities of real life. The first task is to identify all the tasks that have to be completed, then the length of time they will take and the dependencies between tasks.

Table 6.1 *Schedule of tasks and time*

Task	Days	Relationships
A	3	must complete first
B	12	after A, before F
C	3	after A, before F
D	4	after A, before F
E	2	after A, before F
F	1	after A to E
TOTAL	25	

This schedule requires 25 days in total. However, the project could be completed in 16 days if tasks C to E were undertaken in parallel with B. Even if C to E were undertaken sequentially, they would still be completed before B. With only one person available for all tasks, the full 25 days would be needed, but if tasks can be allocated between two or more people, it will reduce to the lower figure.

If time is critical, we might want to examine task B to see if additional resources could be applied to reduce its time. Is it the sort of task that could be split up between two people? By reducing the total time for B to six days we would then need to ensure that tasks C and D were handled simultaneously, so that tasks C to E would also take only six days. Figure 6.2 shows the network diagram that could be drawn from the schedule. For a problem as small as this, it is as easy to use the schedule. However, imagine a project with several hundred tasks and the advantages of network analysis will be clear.

The method illustrated in simple terms here is commonly called CPA or CPM (critical path analysis/method). A more sophisticated method is PERT (programme evaluation and

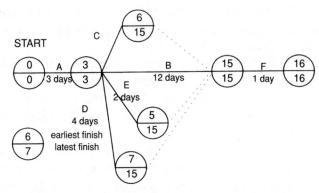

If C, D and E could only be performed sequentially, and B took only 6 days, the network would look somewhat different, and the critical path would change:

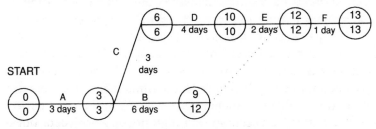

There are many variants of network diagrams, and the examples gives some idea of how the technique might be used.

Figure 6.2 *Example of a network diagram*

review technique). This begins in a similar way, a main difference being in how the durations of activities are estimated. PERT has three calculations for each activity: the most likely duration, and optimistic and pessimistic estimates. Probability analysis is then used to calculate an expected time. This method can change perceptions of the critical path. Both methods can be extended to incorporate costs and resources.

common pitfalls to avoid in project management

1. The organization may fail to identify all the tasks that

have to be undertaken if it lacks experience in the management of a particular change. In very complex situations this can be a vital issue.

2. Perhaps the most common fault is to under-estimate the amount of time that a task will take. This may be because the manager knows the actual time needed but forgets to allow for the time requirements of the normal job or for the response time from customers, suppliers or colleagues. It may take only a two-hour meeting to deal with one aspect, but if all the people you need to meet are busy it may be several days before you can get them together. Inexperience also makes time assessment difficult.

3. Forgetting multiple demands on management time. If there is only one project drawing resources from the organization, it may not be too difficult to assess resource requirements against needs. In fundamental change there may be several simultaneous projects, each putting demands on the same managers. To solve this problem there needs to be an overall co-ordination of all the projects so that high priority projects receive high priority treatment.

4. If the volume of work in managing the change is beyond the resources of the organization. It might be desirable to examine whether the changes can be phased, on the basis that doing each phase well will bring a better result than trying to do too much and not achieving the desired change because of this.

5. Control over suppliers. Problems of time estimation and control become harder when some of the tasks are undertaken by suppliers, such as sub-contractors in a construction project. Under modern conditions where outsourcing has been extended, there may be many more organizations and people to work with in order to manage a project.

ensuring

Ensuring is the process of monitoring and control to keep the implementation actions on track. Organizations have control systems, but these are not always adequate for monitoring major abnormal circumstances because the information collected, the regularity of reports and the way reports are written may be totally inappropriate for controlling change processes. Each of the implementation approaches discussed earlier can provide the basis of a control system. However, management control is about more than policing, and there are many behavioural aspects.

goal congruence

1. Are all the controls and incentives driving the organi-zation in the same direction? Check that the require-ments from the change process are not being frustrated by requirements elsewhere in the organization.
2. Are the personal aims of the key people in the change process and the organizational goals in harmony? The organization will achieve things more quickly where congruence exists.
3. How far can self-control be used as a driving force in this change? When there is total identification with the goals, the self-discipline of the individual may be a more powerful drive than the formal control system.
4. Share the vision. Exercise the controls in ways that increase the degree to which the vision and strategies for the change are shared by all involved. For example, engender enthusiastic discussion of overall progress, as well as examination of individual responsibilities.
5. Use the control process for the change as a learning opportunity as far as possible, and as a way of over-coming new challenges that emerge as the change is managed. This philosophy does not mean that indivi-

duals who do not do the things promised without good reason should not be held to account. However, if the whole team is motivated to achieve the change, the emphasis should not be on who we should blame but how we overcome obstacles.

designing the control system for the change process

1. Two facets require regular, timely flows of information: did we do the things we said we would at the right time; did the outcome of those actions achieve our expectations?
2. Ensure that information flows are set up to monitor critical elements of the change. It is usually easier to check that an action has been taken than whether it achieved the desired results. For example, if the action is a conference to help change the organization's culture, a relatively simple administrative process will ensure feedback on whether the conference was held. Assessing its effectiveness will require much more work, such as surveys before and after the event.
3. Ensure that the control system does more than pass information along. Establish regular control meetings, so that any necessary re-planning can take place. Create an environment where people find out the reasons for deviations before coming to meetings, and do not waffle or simply guess at the reasons for deviation: openness and honesty are essential.
4. Bring all control information for the process together regularly, so that the person with overall responsibility for managing the change is not taken by surprise.
5. Pay particular attention to those tasks that will delay the project if they are not performed to time. Delays may do more than hold up the process: they can lead

to morale problems as people become aware of the change before the organization is in a position to explain it or deal with the personal issues that arise.

6. The normal control processes of the organization might not be adequate to monitor the change. Check them out and, if necessary, set up some temporary procedures for the duration of the change project. An example is that when setting a project budget it is important to make sure that the internal accounting system can cope with it. If the whole accounting system is geared to providing information by expense and revenue headings under hierarchical responsibility centres, it may not be possible for it to provide management information on a project basis. For the project budget to be used for control, it would be necessary for an alternative method of monitoring the budget to be put in place.

7. Accept that things will go wrong and that quick response is therefore vital. Ensure that the quick response is not just a knee jerk reaction, which means properly understanding what has gone wrong before trying to put it right.

8. Understand that some expense may have to be incurred to monitor and control the project. It may be that a change project can be fully monitored from the existing management information system, but it is more likely that additional methods will be needed. There is a cost to these.

recognition

Recognition is an important part of the management process. In this section I argue that the non-monetary aspects of recognition are the most important in building an organization that will successfully negotiate the change. One example of non-monetary recognition was given by the president of Premier to the task force, whose work was described in the previous chapter. An award was made annually to the team that made the greatest contribution to the progress and development of the organization. This is known inside the company as the president's gold medal award. This award was given to the task force when the success of their activities became apparent:

1. Give constant recognition to the parts others play as the change process moves forward.
2. Use opportunities to reinforce the behaviour you want from others, by making them feel that what they are doing is important and has been noticed.
3. Take opportunities to acknowledge publicly the genuine achievements of others in aiding the change process. Do not make negative comments about anyone in public, although you should discuss your criticisms with the person in a private meeting.
4. Make sure that your superiors are aware of outstanding performance by others, and that your team knows that you are not taking all the credit for efforts they have shared.
5. Do not indulge in empty praise and insincere comments.
6. Have regular personal performance reviews for people who are reporting to you during the change process, so that you both have the opportunity to develop relationships and avoid surprises.

two loose ends

The task of thinking about the EASIER model is not quite over, and there are two issues that do not fit under any one heading of the model but which nevertheless are very important: the problem of stress and the management of survivors of change.

stress

Stress arises from events and situations in the environment of an individual that cause adverse psychological and psychosomatic reactions. Of course, stress also arises from situations outside the work place, as well as from the normal process of working and interfacing with other people. Under normal conditions stress is experienced regularly. A combination of events might include: a dispute with a family member before setting out for work; a late, overcrowded train with delays on the journey to work; a phone call from an unhappy customer, followed by a sharp word from a colleague; and an unpleasant interview with the boss. This could leave some people at explosion point. Any one of these factors might be shrugged off; however, as a combination, they have the potential to raise stress levels too high. Under normal conditions the same sequence of events is not expected to happen every day, so few people are in a permanent state of stress. Of course it can happen, even in an unchanging environment, if people are always overworked, are in a job that they are not fully competent to do or are bullied, as well as from many other causes. However, it is not stress in general that concerns us here, but stress arising from a change situation.

In any fundamental change, stress can be expected to increase: when people have to behave differently, work in a different way, if they have to work longer, and particularly if their livelihoods are under a real or perceived threat. Those leading a change are also put under considerable stress, particularly if resistance to the change is high and the penalties of failure are great. How much stress increases depends on the differences between individuals (we do not all suffer stress over the same things, or to the same extent), and the way in which the change is managed. You can often see living proof of the different behaviour caused by stress by observing fellow passengers at an airport when a charter flight is delayed indefinitely. Some appear to avoid stress, settle back with a book, and take the attitude that as they can do nothing about it there is no point getting agitated. Others become tense, cannot settle, and keep looking at the indicator boards, even though they may have been told that nothing would happen for at least four hours. Others become aggressive, pick arguments with the ground staff of the airline, and may become personally abusive, even though most would know intellectually that the ground staff had not delayed the plane and could not do anything to hurry it up.

Prolonged severe stress can lead to heart attacks and mental illness, and, even if it does not reach these extremes, may cause irritability, depression, and general unhappiness. The results of continued high levels of stress may be lack of attention to work, time off for illness, disruptive personal behaviour, and other actions that are in the interests of neither the organization nor the employee.

Although no one can remove all the causes of stress from a change situation, the way the change is managed can raise or reduce stress levels. Every manager who is either leading a change or playing a part in the change process has a duty to the shareholders to act in the best interests of the firm, and to the employees to manage in a humane and caring way.

some management actions that increase stress

- Announcing changes piecemeal, instead of as a total plan. A long chain of serious changes, particularly if they threaten people's security, can keep an organization in a state of unhealthy tension. Sometimes, as in a turnaround situation, this may be inevitable, although I am not convinced that this is inevitably so. It is a question of getting a clarity of vision that reaches the causes of the problem, rather than just reacting to symptoms as they are observed.

- Allow people to learn about changes from rumour or the press. Management must tell the affected people before they get the news from elsewhere. Action should be taken to counteract erroneous rumours, which means careful attention to communication throughout the change process.

■ Refusing to explain the reason for the changes. More tension is caused if people feel resentful about a change: sometimes this may be because they do not understand that it is necessary.

■ Not giving the organization a vision of where the changes will lead. This can leave people without hope that things will improve.

■ Increasing uncertainty by leaving long delays between announcing a change and telling people affected what it will mean to them. The shorter the process, the less will be the period of worry.

■ Telling lies. If people find that management is not straight with them, every statement made in the future will be reinterpreted in a worse light.

I am sure that you could add to this list of ways not to behave. In addition to acting in the opposite way to that described, there are some other positive ways a manager can help to reduce stress.

some management behaviour that may reduce stress

■ Try to see things from the viewpoint of the people who are affected by the change. If the manager is empathetic to those affected, solutions are more likely to be found that reduce levels of concern and worry.

■ Involve those affected whenever possible. Participation has been discussed elsewhere. All that needs to be added is that when people feel they are making some of the choices, they are more likely to feel positively about the change.

■ Support those affected. Support has been discussed as part of the EASIER model. In this context it means making time to listen to the concerns of individuals, providing counselling where needed, and making sure that if job content changes the individuals have the skills and competencies to equip them for the new situation.

■ Treat all genuine concerns seriously. Even if you think a concern raised is trivial, deal with it in a serious way. It may not be trivial to the person who has raised it.

■ Communicate, communicate, communicate. Frequent and honest communication, particularly two-way communication, builds trust, and a high trust in a manager will do much to remove many unfounded perceptions that would otherwise add to stress.

management of survivors of change

Not all change involves people losing their jobs with the organization, but much of it does. If people were chess pieces, some would be swept off the board, while the survivors would carry on, unemotionally accepting that each had more ground to cover. They would happily move to different areas of the board as required, and if necessary would be sacrificed for the greater good. Although some managers have been known to plan change as if people were no more than inanimate objects in the corporate game, this is not the surest route to success.

Those of us who do not treat people as chess pieces have little difficulty in feeling empathy with those who are compelled to leave the organization. It is very easy to put ourselves in their shoes, even if we ourselves have never had that experience.

What may be less obvious is that the survivors who remain with the organization frequently do not have great feelings of devotion and gratitude towards the organization because they have been spared. Because a change has not been implemented until the organization has digested the new situation or methods, and is working effectively, attention to the reactions of survivors may be a critical factor.

Survivors' reactions are affected by a number of variables, which include:

- The extent to which the redundancies were expected and the reasons explained and accepted as justified, in which case reactions may be more favourable than if the change was a bolt from the blue.
- The way in which the redundancies were announced. Even when the reasons for the redundancy are understood, negative feelings may be generated by the way in which the announcement was handled. These persist, even after the departure of those who had to leave.
- How fair the selection procedures appeared to the survivors. Reactions are likely to be more adverse if the procedure seems to be unfair. Voluntary redundancy is likely to cause fewer adverse reactions than compulsory selection.
- The degree to which the jobs of survivors and leavers are interdependent. The closer they are, the more the survivors will identify with those who have to leave. People will not be as concerned about things that are happening in an unconnected division of the company, or in another country, as they are about the departure of close colleagues, or a section of the organization with whom they have regular dealings.
- How closely those leaving resemble those staying in skills and attitudes. We identify more with people like ourselves than with those we see as very different. For example, shop assistants in a large retail group are unlikely to identify strongly if employment levels in the head office buying department are reduced, whereas those in the buying department who remain, and others at head office who identify with them, may have strong reactions.
- How insecure the survivors feel, which is related to the

chances that those who leave have of finding other jobs, the personal experiences of previous redundancies by those who survive, and any perception that this is just the first of a whole sequence of redundancies that are due to occur. The higher the insecurity, the greater will be the adverse reactions of the survivors.

■ The level of attention given to helping the survivors to cope with the new situation, where the redundancies mean that the survivors have to work in a different way or apply different skills and competencies. However, reactions will be more severe if the survivors feel that they have been thrown into the deep end and expected to find their own way out, whether or not they can swim.

Attitudes and feelings of survivors manifest themselves in behaviour. Typical attitudes and feelings that survivors may experience include:

■ guilt that they have not lost their jobs when other equally good people have had to go;
■ disbelief and a sense of betrayal ('they would not do this to us', followed by 'how could they do this to us?');
■ anger and animosity, which can be either open or suppressed;
■ lack of commitment, low morale, and insecurity.

These can convert into absenteeism, lack of initiative, resignations of people the organization needs to keep, and poorer performance. In turn, such attitudes can lead to increased stress and genuine illness among at least some of the survivors. It is all very much like resistance to change, except that the survivors are not resisting, they are reacting to the change. They have no hope of turning the clock back to prevent the change.

It is not possible to remove every negative feeling, but effective management of change in such situations can reduce many of them. There are many points where the manager is able to affect the outcome by the actions he or she takes:

- ▉ Expectations of survivors can be managed by giving an awareness of the underlying problem. This is most easily achieved when the organization has an established briefing process, so that good and bad news that affects the employees are shared on a regular basis.
- ▉ A vision of what the changes will mean for the future should be provided so that some of the uncertainty of survivors is removed. We have met this several times before.
- ▉ Announcements can be made in a manner that does not shock or leave the impression that the organization does not care about those sacked.
- ▉ Redundancies can be handled in a way that is not only fair, but is seen to be fair.
- ▉ Employees can be given coaching and training to help them ease into their new roles.
- ▉ Attention can be given to the legitimate concerns of survivors. This means listening to what these are and, where possible, taking action to deal with them. Where they cannot be removed, the manager can at least ensure that the individuals know why.
- ▉ Advice and help can be given to assist those made redundant in finding new jobs. Survivors do not directly benefit from this, but it demonstrates to them that the organization cares about those it has made redundant. Such actions can be of real benefit to those leaving, and a source of comfort to those remaining.

managing corporate wide change when you are not the managing director

working from the middle

It is easy to see how all the points covered in the book so far can be applied when the change starts from the top of the organization. The CSA and BP were among the many examples of change that started from this point, although the CSA was somewhat unusual as it was a change that began with the setting up of a new organization. It is not too difficult to see how a manager at any level can apply the methods covered, provided the changes affect only that manager's area of responsibility. There may be a need to obtain a higher level approval for some types of change, but by and large it is possible to use the ideas at any level in the organization.

In this section we should think about another source of change: any manager who is initiating a change that will impact on other areas of the organization, which are outside of his or her sphere of responsibility. Such a change could be a new process or system, the removal of a service once supplied to other managers, or the adoption of a new product concept. The manager in charge of customer relations might want to make sweeping changes to how customers were dealt with, the levels of service provided, and overall attitudes to customers. Could this be achieved on his or her own authority alone? The answer is probably no, because so many other parts of the organization would also have to change. This is the sort of situation that requires some additional thought and effort.

We saw a hint of this in the Premier Foods case in Chapter 5. However, my involvement in that case was as managing director of the management consultancy chosen by Premier to help with this change, so there are some aspects about which I do not have detailed information. For this reason, I am setting out a fictitious case that can be used as a vehicle to help explore some of the issues in this type of situation.

---

example: Illusory Enterprises plc: A

Ann Meadows had recently joined Illusory as training and development manager at corporate head office. She was 30, well qualified, and highly motivated to make a personal contribution to the organization. She was responsible for all internal training courses, and approving applications to attend external courses.

The training and development manager reported to a manager of HRM (human resources management), who in turn reported to a director of administration. Her immediate boss was in his late forties and somewhat conservative in his ways. He had been in the organization for nearly 20 years, and had been in his present position for 10 years, having previously been the training and development manager. Ann was to find that HRM was tolerated rather than admired within the organization.

Within the HR department Ann had a number of colleagues, theoretically at peer level, although it was obvious that some were more equal than others. Most influential was Nick Smith, to whom the bulk of people in the department reported. There were two other peer managers. Although there were personnel officers at each of the three sites occupied by the three business units of the company, training was centralized. If a managing director of a business unit (who would also be a member of the executive committee and the main board) required a specific course he would call in the training and development manager to discuss it. There was also a small steering group with a representative from each of the business units, which monitored training activity and agreed the scope of any new course that seemed to be indicated from needs identified from the annual appraisal process. The representatives in this group tended to be the personnel officers, though this had been not the intention when it was set up 12 years ago.

Ann had a staff of four training officers, two administrators, and a departmental secretary. Although many in-house courses were designed and run by the training officers, there were a number that were run by consultants and colleges, most of these outside providers being associates of long standing. The company system was that in-house courses were advertised in an internal programme, in written form and on an internal web site. Individuals either chose the course themselves and applied to attend or were asked to attend as a result of the annual appraisal; in either case their application had to be supported by their departmental manager. Prices were set for each course place and charged to the business units and departments sending participants, the aim being for training and development to make neither a surplus nor a loss during each year. Travel and accommodation costs of those attending were paid by the participants and reclaimed from their departments on expense claims. One result of this was that the full costs of training were not collated in any central place and so were unknown.

As she settled into her new job, Ann began to feel that what was currently going on was not in the best interests of the organization. Most training effort seemed to be directed at lower levels in the organization, and very few of the more senior middle managers and above ever attended anything. Line managers were neutral about training, and would often disrupt a course by pulling out participants because of a minor problem. There had been very few changes to the content of courses from when they were first set up. Most people who attended were volunteers, and the people for whose needs the courses had been designed rarely came. There was no follow up on the impacts of the training on either job performance or company results. In fact although most of the training was of high quality, little of it addressed corporate priorities. There was a problem in that Ann did not know the corporate priorities in detail, though she did know that little of what was being done matched the vision statement or the recent announcement she had read in the press that the company was looking for a major expansion into the United States and several European countries, where it currently had no business activity.

Something had to change. Ann felt that an urgent and fundamental shake up was needed, to give training a business driven focus.

How would you begin the task of changing things if you were Ann?

her initial options

Ann has authority to make incremental changes, but she has a fundamental shake up in mind. She is at the stage when she sees a need for change, but has not worked out precisely what is needed to replace the existing system. At this stage she does not know the extent of resistance to any significant changes, and she also has a number of different individuals to consider:

■ Her boss, who we know is conservative and also once ran her department. He may well be very resistant.

■ Her more than equal peer colleague, who seems to

have influence with her boss, some of whose activities may be affected by any change in Ann's area.

■ Her other peer colleagues in HRM, who may also find some of their activities affected.

■ Her own staff, who appear to be content to continue doing what they are doing.

■ The personnel officers, who almost by default are members of the steering committee.

■ The chief executives and key managers in the business units, who appear somewhat unsupportive of training.

■ Heads of other staff units, about whom we know nothing.

■ The chief executive, particularly if the changes mean that Ann must have access to more strategic information, or require more resources to be spent on training and development.

■ The rest of the organization, whose opposition for the most part would not block any changes, though there might be some key people who would have more influence and who might be more critical in successful implementation of the change.

At the stage where she now is, Ann would probably find it easy to gain general support from her boss and colleagues that she should review what is going on, and come up with ideas. It is the sort of decision that carries no risk, even to the most conservative manager.

Ann has a number of options over the next step that must enable her to be able to set out the present state of affairs. She must understand the reason why change is necessary, and have a clear vision of that change and of the initial things that must be done to move to a different outcome:

■ She could continue to work on it without involving others.

■ She could make it a joint project with the people who report to her.

- She could use the existing steering group to work on this stage.
- She could make up a task force, including some line managers, some HR specialists and, perhaps, one of two of her staff.
- She might decide that a consulting firm might best fulfil this phase of the work, not because she in unable to do it, but for internal credibility and political reasons.

Think for a moment which route you would take. Or would you do something completely different? Before I suggest my view, I should like to introduce two new thoughts: the value of gaining a champion in situations like this, and the risks which research shows that specialist units can run if they do not take care during the investigatory phase.

gaining a champion

You may recall that the Premier case mentioned that there was a high level champion of the change, although there was little indication of what that person did, or why the role was of value. Champions are most frequently referred to in books about innovation, and it is easy to think of them in connection with new products. I like the definition of innovation used by a former colleague, Beth Webster:

> Simply put, 'innovation' is a better thing to do, or a better way to do it, that increases an organization's ability to achieve its goals. This does not mean change for change's sake. To qualify as an innovation, a change must be visible to others and must offer a lasting impact.

Ann's vision would qualify as an innovation, it would have a corporate wide effect, yet her ability to implement it, or even to get top management agreement to start, is limited by her position in the hierarchy. If she had great charisma, a strong track record in the company, and therefore great personal credibility, she might be able to get the changes going on her own. But she is new, and has yet to establish her credibility. Consequently, she needs to find a champion who will fight her corner at top management level, and with line managers. The following quotation sums up the role of the champion:

> Champions are individuals who take on an idea (theirs or that of an idea generator) for a new product or service and do all they can within their power to ensure the success of the innovation. By actively promoting the idea, communicating and inspiring others with their vision of the potential of the innovation, champions can help the organization realize the potential of an innovation.
>
> (Afuah, 1998)

The author goes on to argue that recognition of the potential may lead to internal coalitions to oppose it! Therefore, it is important that the champion has the power and prestige within the organization to be able to fight these coalitions.

From this we can distil the characteristics of the champion that Ann will need to help her implement the change she is beginning to formulate:

■ political clout;
■ high credibility within the organization;
■ access to top and senior management (ideally from the ranks of the top management team);
■ willingness to put his/her reputation on the line;
■ determination;
■ change leadership skills.

Ann's boss does not appear to be a good champion candidate. If HRM is not held in high regard, and he himself is conservative, he is unlikely to fit the bill, and in any case he is not a member of the inner circle of the organization. She will need his support, but could not rely on him to get her vision into the areas where it mattered. To get his support, she might be advised to look closely at Nick Smith. The case does not tell us much about him. If his influence with her boss is cronyism rather than ability, he might be a broken reed. But if he has genuine influence through ability, credibility and personality, he may well be a useful ally who she will need to get on her side.

The director of administration might be a logical choice of champion, but if HRM has little credibility, and he is responsible for it, there may be a problem. Again, she does not want him to be hostile, but he may not be the right person for the champion role.

From her position she would only be likely to get easy access to the chief executive of the whole company if he had initiated the change process, which in this case he had not. To try to get regular access to him would mean going over the heads of the two people above her, which could be politically damaging to her. There may be a planning director, who might have the necessary qualifications, and his interest might be if Ann's concepts were an aid to the implementation of strategies. So he is a possibility.

However, a better option might be one of the managing directors of the business units, if she can get one on her side. The fact that she has access to these people through her job makes it possible to find whether they share her concerns that training could be a greater contributor to bottom line results. Even at this stage, she has enough of a vision of what it might do to test the enthusiasm of each of these people. If she can get the managing director with the greatest personal credibility on her side, she has a good possibility of getting a strong champion for the change.

Without being in her shoes, we could not take the choice of champion any further. But the discussion has helped us look at the important role that a champion could play in a change situation of this type.

specialist task forces

Professor Andrew Pettigrew, in 1975 ('Strategic aspects of the management of specialists activity', *Personnel Review*, **4**, November), drew attention to a typical cycle that new specialist units often went through. His study covered new specialist units, and all those in the sample were set up following either an internal political drama, or as a response to external events. The sponsor of the initiative recruits a new manager, who in turn sets up and manages a specialist team, many of whom also are recruited from outside the organization. One characteristic of the organizations he studied was that the new unit had been set up as 'a sudden unplanned act of creation'. He called this the conception phase.

During the next phase, pioneering, the new group sets to with great enthusiasm, usually with a high involvement and commitment to the group. Often the togetherness of the group leads them to appear different from the rest of the organization, in dress, language or behaviour. Sometimes the group is located separately from the mainstream of business activity. Frequently the new manager takes on a barrier role to shield the group from the pressures of the organization.

Within the group there is often a division of thinking between the strategists and pragmatists. The former want to get everything right for the long-term; the latter argue that an immediate success is necessary for credibility, and the long-term process would then take care of itself. Initially the tensions created by these divisions stimulate problem solving, where the pragmatists tend to dominate, but inevitably the divisions contribute to the next phase, self-doubt.

Self-doubt begins when the process of diagnosis is completed and plans for the new process affecting the whole organization are unveiled to an unsuspecting organization:

> Because the process of diagnosis has been largely consultant centred and not client centred, with a great deal of the specialist's linkage being

with their political sponsor and much of the important synthesizing of the diagnostic data going on in the closed walls of the specialist unit, there are many surprises in the initial reports. Some groups in the organization may suddenly find themselves confronted by specialists of whose existence they had been in virtual ignorance.

An immediate result is hostility to the changes, fuelled by a feeling of being threatened. This may be exacerbated if the original political sponsor has by this time moved on, or appears to be less that fully supportive.

Pettigrew found that all the specialist units he studied tended to over-perceive the degree of threat posed to its existence by the reactions. This was often also influenced by an immediate decline in the previous heavy workload, and concerns over personal futures. There was often a growing feeling of rejection of the leader of the unit by the previously highly motivated team. In effect, the unit fuels its own feelings of uncertainty instead of managing some of the original causes of doubt.

The self-doubt phase may be of little further consequence to the behaviour of members of the unit if it was in any case intended to have a planned demise on completion of the report. However, the changes recommended, which may well be in the best interests of the organization, may wither and die with the unit.

Pettigrew found that where there was no planned demise, the groups took one of two courses: maladaptive and adaptive.

Typical of maladaptive responses are:

■ reacting to the symptoms of problems instead of their causes;

■ withdrawing from sources of pressure instead of facing up to them;

■ avoiding risk, and therefor failing to build the credibility of the group;

■ hardening lines of difference within the unit, and between the unit and the organization;

■ behaviour becoming destructive within the unit, and a culture of blame developing.

The depth and strength of these responses will of course vary. Typical outcomes are the collapse of the unit, or its absorption into another area of the organization, and in both of these cases the hoped-for change, which was the reason for the formation of the unit in the first place, is unlikely to be carried out.

The other possibility is for the unit to follow a strategy of adaptive responses, which are concerned with building processes and relationships in a way that seeks to understand and confront the causes of self doubt and rejection. These responses include:

■ diagnosing the real causes of self doubt;
■ developing widespread linkages with the rest of the organization;
■ gaining access to important policy committees;
■ decentralizing, by either splitting up the work of the unit and physically locating some members of the unit in user departments, or setting up project teams that have members from other groups in the organization;
■ ensuring that the physical location of the group facilitates informal contact with the organization.

The keynotes to this approach to strategy management are diagnosis and anticipation, not carried out unilaterally, but in relation to the needs and experiences of its potential and actual clients.

Adaptive approaches often result in a successful outcome for the unit. However, an even better approach is to avoid the pitfalls by using approaches such as these from the beginning, ensuring that there is wide awareness of the unit and the progress it is making, so that many of the potential obstacles never arise.

Ann's situation is a little different from the units in the research study. Although she is new, her unit is not. When a manager comes into a department with revolutionary new ideas, there is sometimes a reaction from the people in the department. Some like it, and switch to the new thinking with great enthusiasm. Others are hostile, and may well leave of their own accord, to be replaced by new recruits who are believers in the new cause. Some may put their heads down, and hope that the whole issue goes away. It is by no means an unlikely scenario that someone in Ann's situation might within a few months be working with a very different team under her.

The lessons from the research can easily be carried over to the formation of task forces to aid the diagnostic stages of an intended change. Flip back to the choices Ann had about her next steps, and think about what you would do in her situation in the light of the points made about specialist units and champions. My recommendation is incorporated into the second part of the case study.

---

example: Illusory Enterprises plc: B

Ann was well aware that, unless she could envision the proposed change and then get others to share that vision through her activating activities, her revolutionary ideas had little chance of success. She rejected the idea of using consultants, because she saw difficulty in securing funding for their services, and because she knew how to undertake the necessary diagnostic work. In any case, she felt that this would be begging the question, as when they reported she would still be left with all the problems of implementation.

Her first step was to obtain agreement from her boss that she should set up a working party to undertake a review of her function and its activities. She did not disclose all her expectations from this review at this stage, and used more general arguments, such as 'strategic', 'ensuring greater effectiveness', 'client centred', and 'responsiveness to the organization's needs'.

Before doing this she talked things over in broad terms with Nick Smith, voicing more of her concerns about what she had discovered so far. He agreed that he would play a personal role in any task force she might set up. Her approach made it harder for her conservative boss to say no than to say yes, particularly as she was able to say that Nick had agreed to be involved. In any case, as she was entitled to undertake such a review using her own people, a decision to widen the task force was not too difficult for her boss to take.

She next went to each of the managing directors of the business units to ask them to support the task force by each appointing one senior manager to work on it. She found that none of them were very satisfied with the current state of training. One in particular, James Kerridge, seemed excited by any move to make the process more strategic and more client centred. Ann took the opportunity to ask if she could obtain his advice from time to time as the work progressed, as she was still very new to the company and could use all the help she could get.

The task force now consisted of five people, including her, and was linked to the businesses and to other areas of HRM. Ann felt that this gave opportunities to develop stronger links with the businesses. She intended to use people from her own department as a flexible working party, bringing them into the task force deliberations from time to time. Her own staff were to be kept informed about every aspect of the work, and she talked about progress with them at least once every day when they were in the office, and periodically as a group.

The task force had four tasks:

■ to assess what was happening at present, and to obtain and analyse factual evidence so that the current state could be made clear to all;
■ to develop a clear vision statement of what the organization should do, assuming changes were indicated;

- ■ to state a broad outline of the policies and principles that would be needed to support the vision;
- ■ to demonstrate the benefits and cost implications of the new vision.

Ann used the members of the working party to gain access to a wide variety of people during the information collection stage. Among the initiatives she took was a series of discussion meetings with the senior management of each business unit, to obtain their perspective on what they felt they wanted. She or her training officers held focus group meetings with people at all levels, to get feedback on training activities from a participant viewpoint.

She and Nick gave regular feedback to their boss and, as things developed to the director of administration. However, her boss prevented her from seeking direct access to the chief executive.

The information and analysis stage gave full support to her earlier, less complete investigations. One of the things done was to identify training activities under the following broad headings, showing the proportion of training time under each. The headings and percentages were:

1. Tied into corporate vision, policy, and strategy, where some results could be measured: 1%.
2. For the general good of the organization, but with somewhat longer-term benefits, which are harder to validate (for example, induction programmes and developing people for promotion): 5%.
3. Improving immediate individual job performance: 10%.
4. Identified from personal needs appraisals, but having little obvious connection to what the organization needs: 35%.
5. Meeting individual requests, with little apparent value to the organization: 49%.

The vision statement and supporting outline policies and principles would require the organization to make many major changes. Among the main points were:

- ■ A clear statement that the main priority of training was to contribute to business success.
- ■ An intention to use training to aid the implementation of business needs.
- ■ No internal courses would be run under categories 4 and 5 above; instead the company would establish a learning centre with various distance learning materials, and open to all employees. Materials would be available on loan for personal study at home.
- ■ Some of the subjects in category 4 might be repositioned within a higher priority course.
- ■ Categories 1, 2 and 3 would each take up a third of total time spent on courses.
- ■ Category 1 courses would where necessary cascade from top to bottom of the relevant areas of the firm.
- ■ Attendance at category 1 and 3 courses would be made compulsory for those selected.
- ■ There would be follow up activities after every training course to assess results.
- ■ A new steering committee would be established for training, which would include appropriate members of the executive committee.

There was much more than this, but the critical point was that the changes would have an effect on the whole organization.

The task force was unanimous in its endorsement of the new approach, and a meeting was arranged to gain the commitment of the business unit managing directors. Ann had wanted to invite the whole executive committee, including the chief executive, but her boss refused this request. On the day, she was surprised to find the whole of the executive committee there. James Kerridge had persuaded his fellow managing directors that this was important, and they had invited the rest of the executive. In fact, James was so supportive at the meeting that the director of administration felt compelled to give it his backing.

Towards the end of the meeting James said that it would obviously take some time for the whole of the new approach to be implemented. However, in the meantime, he would like a pilot course designed to help him implement the strategy for his business area, and the first people to attend would be himself and his senior managers.

You may not agree with everything Ann did, and you may well see some other things that she should have done. What should be clear is that she was trying to avoid the trap of a task force that exploded its work into the organization without first gaining legitimacy and credibility. At the same time she was building a relationship with the business units that was much stronger than she could have achieved without the task force. This led to her gaining the support of one managing director, who became willing to act as a champion for the changes.

There are some areas where she has not been quite as adept, and which could cause problems. Although she has the most influential of her HRM colleagues involved, the same cannot be said of the other two HR managers, whom she seems to have ignored. There are also the people who report to these managers, including the personnel officers who had a role in the steering committee but played no part in her task force. Furthermore, creating a sense of excitement within HRM could have built up pressure on her boss to be more supportive.

She has built up some potential problems with her boss and the director of administration, who appear to have been manoeuvred into apparent support. However, although this may have removed the immediate hurdle, there will be a chain of decisions as the change is implemented where resentment could cause them to frustrate some of the actions she needs to take. It is almost impossible for someone in Ann's position to gain extra budgetary commitments without the backing of the head of department and the responsible director. So we can argue that she should have done more to convert these two people before the big meeting, and this would have been easier had she gained the overt support of the rest of HRM.

She did involve her own department, but may not have thought through the effect of the changes on them as individuals. The new approaches would take them into a different design of training course, much more related to company problems and issues, and in addition most would be working with much more senior managers than hitherto. In turn this could give them concerns about whether they could do this job, worry about the abandonment of some of the courses they were good at running, and stress over their own prospects for continued employment. More support would be needed here, including possibly workshops on the new skills and competencies that would be needed. Lack of morale in her area would feed to other areas of HRM and, through the courses, to other employees. And this could damage the progress being made.

Finally, she seems to have ignored all the support departments in the organization, like finance and planning. This could have been because there was no one there who was critical to her plans. In similar situations, the starting point is the people who can say 'yes'. Once these have been identified, the next step is to see who can say 'no', and there are usually many more of these. Finally, who has influence and could disrupt or argue against the vision in the corridors, dining rooms and boardrooms? Some attention is needed to each of these groups.

In these early stages, Ann has been using the envisioning and activating parts of the EASIER model. (As shown above, the support part should have also been used.) The implications of the change have been carefully analysed, and information obtained that will be useful in the implementation, ensuring and recognition aspects, which only became possible after the meeting with the executive.

A manager in Ann's situation can rarely use charismatic, coercive or dictatorial means to move a personal vision to something that is accepted by the top management of the organization. In her case, the high-level resistance to her ideas at senior management level mainly came from the management of HRM. Line managers who were hostile to training responded to a more business and client centred approach, and their resistance levels dropped. In real situations there are a wide variety of possible situations, and some might be more difficult to resolve than those faced by Ann.

Once the decision-makers accepted the new vision, Ann's position changed. Numerous people will be affected: some may resent losing the opportunity to gain access to courses whenever they felt like it. Others who have successfully dodged attendance at any courses may worry about their personal deficiencies being exposed when attendance becomes compulsory (of course, not everyone in this category will have dodged training for these reasons). Some middle managers may be concerned that it will not be as easy to pull people off courses.

Although part of the change process will become coercive, through new rules and policies, the visionary element is still important. It is also possible, in Anne's situation, for her to gain commitment by selective involvement. For example, although the replacement of some courses by a learning centre becomes an announced decision, consultation is possible with managers and users on what this centre should provide.

In a sense, top management agreement to the new vision now means that the EASIER model can be used to the full, with the advantage that in gaining this agreement there has also been a gain in senior level supporters who will share in the change management process.

choosing the path for change

This chapter provides a decision path for you when involved in a change situation. All the concepts have been described earlier and the path is set out as a checklist of questions to consider, the answers to which should affect how you handle the change situation.

chapter 1

1. Have you thoroughly understood the drivers for change?
2. What type of change are you facing: incremental (go to question 3) or fundamental (go to question 4)?
3. How should you approach the incremental change, having regard to urgency and the amount of resistance you expect to encounter?

■ High urgency/low resistance   Focused participation
■ Low urgency/low resistance   Extensive participation
■ Low urgency/high resistance   Persuasive
■ High urgency/high resistance   Persuasive/coercive
   (go to question 5)

4. How should you approach the fundamental change, having regard to the urgency and the degree of resistance you expect to encounter?

■ High urgency/low resistance   Visionary/charismatic
■ Crisis/low resistance   Visionary/persuasive
■ High urgency/high resistance   Visionary/coercive
■ Crisis/high resistance   Dictatorial

5. Modify your choice of change strategy as a result of your answers to the following:

■ Do those you wish to involve have the ability to participate?
■ Are they motivated to participate?
■ Does the need for confidentiality affect your ability to involve others?
■ Does involvement (or lack of it) fit the culture of the organization?
■ How important is the post-change motivation of employees?

chapter 2

6. For all choices of approach, ensure that you understand the reasons for resistance:

■ What threats are those affected likely to feel?
■ Do you understand the basis of their psychological contracts?
■ Will there be resentment at imposed change?
■ Do they have faith in those making the change?
■ Do you understand the emotional hang-ups?

7. How can you reduce resistance? Consider the value of:

■ Participation
■ Communication
■ Training.

chapter 3

8. For all change situations, have you assessed the implications and effects of the change?
9. Have you used force field analysis or other approaches to think through all aspects of the change?
10. Have you considered all aspects of the integrated organization model, thinking through which elements have to change and how these affect the other elements?

■ The desired change	■ Culture
■ Tasks	■ Information systems
■ People	■ Control systems
■ Structure	■ Reward systems
■ Decision processes	■ Intended results.

chapters 4–6

11. Is your change:

(a) Incremental and with relatively minor impact on the elements of the integrated organization model? If so, move to question 12.
(b) Incremental with a complex impact on the integrated organizational model? If so, move to question 14.
(c) Fundamental? If so, move to question 14.

12.　If your answer to 11 (a) is yes:

■ Have you gone through all the points so far so that you have a clear definition of the change and the way in which it must be implemented?
■ Have you established action plans to implement?
■ Have you set up a way of monitoring progress?

(Note: some help may be obtained from using the management/administrative elements of the EASIER approach to change leadership.)

13.　Good luck, you should be ready to implement.
14.　All other change situations will benefit from the EASIER approach. Are you ready to use the findings from your analysis so far to modify how you use the approach?
15.　Envisioning. Is your vision:

■ Credible?
■ Challenging?
■ Consistent in all parts?
■ Clear?
■ Providing a bridge from the past to the future?
■ Something that you believe in whole-heartedly?

16.　Activating. Have you determined your mix of activating actions?

■ How to demonstrate your own belief in the vision.
■ How you will use personal contact to communicate the vision.
■ Whether to use workshops and conferences.
■ How opportunities for two-way communication can be created.
■ What communication media will be used to support the messages.

- How you can use everyday meetings to build the vision.
- The use of external public relations.
- How you will seek out and use examples of success.
- How to check that training is reinforcing the vision?

17. Support. Have you thought through a strategy for giving support by:

- Expressing confidence in those working with you to implement the change?
- Providing coaching when it is needed?
- Empowering key people?
- Having empathy with those involved in the change?
- Using praise and thanks when appropriate?

18. Implementation. Have you thought through the detailed implementation actions to make the change happen, including:

- Strategies to implement the vision?
- Short-term plans and budgets to turn strategies into action plans?
- Project management for complex situations?

19. Ensuring. How will you monitor and control the change process?
20. Recognition. Have you thought how you will motivate by giving recognition to those playing a part in the change process?
21. Are you emotionally prepared to deal with all the unexpected things that will crop up, and all the matters you should have thought of but overlooked?
22. Have you given thought to how you might reduce the levels of stress that those under you will feel when the change is implemented?

23. Have you given attention to the particular problems of the reactions of survivors, if the change has involved people having to leave the organization?

chapter 7

24. Are you the managing director of your company? (If so, go to point 28.)
25. Does the change you wish to make affect departments other than your own in a fundamental way? (If no to these questions, move to 28.)
26. Does top management already fully support the proposed change? (If so, move to 28.)
27. Have you:

■ A clear understanding of the change?
■ Evidence to support the need for the change?
■ Assessed the levels of support you are likely to receive from your boss and the top management of the firm?
■ Considered the value of finding a champion for the change from the ranks of top management?
■ Examined ways that you can get key managers on your side through participative approaches?
■ Understood the dangers that face a specialist unit that suggests major change, but is otherwise isolated from the organization?
■ Developed a plan for gaining top management commitment to your vision?

28. If you have followed the points through, you should have a comprehensive approach mapped out that will enable you to implement in an effective way. Good luck, but remember that there is a continuous nature to many of the steps, and that some will be repeated. You cannot simply forget each stage once you have undertaken the initial actions you have planned.

further reading

change management and change leadership

Afuah, A (1998) *Innovation Management: strategy, implementation, and profits*, Oxford University Press, New York.

Dinkelspiel, J R and Bailey, J (1991) High performing organizations: aligning culture and organization around strategy, in *International Review of Strategic Management*, ed D E Hussey, vol 2, part 1, Wiley, Chichester.

Hussey, D E, ed (1993) *International Review of Strategic Management*, vol 4, Chapters 2–8, Wiley, Chichester.

Nadler, D A and Tushman, M L (1989) Leadership for Organizational Change, in *Large scale Organizational Change*, eds Morhman et al, Jossey Bass, San Francisco.

Nicholls, J (1999) Value-centred leadership: applying transformational leadership to produce strategic behaviour in depth, in *Strategic Change*, Part 1, 8.6, *Strategic Change*, Part 2, 8.7.

Stace, D A and Dunphy, D C (1992) Translating business strategies into action: managing strategic change, in *Strategic Change*, 1, 2 (reproduced in *The Implementation Challenge*, ed D E Hussey (1996), Wiley, Chichester).

Tichy, N M and Devanna, M A (1982) (1990) *The Transformational Leader*, Wiley, New York.

success and failure in implementation

Hussey, D E, ed (1996) *The Implementation Challenge*, Wiley, Chichester.

Hussey, D E (1997) Strategic management: past experiences and future directions, *Strategic Change*, Part 1, 6.5, *Strategic Change*, Part 2, 6.6.

Kaplan, R (1995) *Building a Management System to Implement your Strategy: strategic management survey*, Renaissance Solutions, London.

Kitching, J (1973) *Acquisitions in Europe: causes of corporate success and failure*, Business International, Geneva.

KPMG (1997) *Colouring in the Map: mergers and acquisitions in Europe*, Research Report, KPMG Consulting, London.

project management

Lock, D (1984) *Project Management*, 3rd edn, Gower, Aldershot.

Young, T L (1998) *The Handbook of Project Management*, Kogan Page, London.

strategic management

Hussey, D E (1998) *Strategic Management: from theory to implementation*, 4th edn, Butterworth-Heinemann, Oxford.

Hussey, D E (1999), *Strategy and Planning*, Wiley, Chichester, 5th edn (first 4 were published under the title *Introducing Corporate Planning*, Pergamon, Oxford).

McNamee, P (1998) *Strategic Market Planning: a blueprint for success*, Wiley, Chichester.